ARK PAPERBACKS

ROMANTIC IMAGE

'In this extremely important book of speculative and scholarly criticism, Mr Kermode is setting out to re-define the notion of the Romantic tradition, especially in its relation to English poetry and criticism. He makes us realise the extraordinary strength of the prolonged trajectory of the Romantic Movement. A rich, packed, suggestive book.' - *TLS*

FRANK KERMODE

One of the leading critics of our day, Frank Kermode writes and broadcasts widely on literary matters. His books include *The Sense of an Ending* (1967), *Shakespeare, Spenser, Donne* (1971), *D. H. Lawrence* (1973), *The Classic* (1975), *The Genesis of Secrecy* (1979) and *Essays on Fiction, 1971–82* (1983). He is a Fellow of King's College, Cambridge, and was until recently Professor of English Literature at Cambridge. He holds honorary degrees from the universities of Chicago and Liverpool, and is a Fellow of the British Academy and of the Royal Society of Literature. He is also an Honorary Foreign Member of the American Academy of Arts and Sciences.

For description of this drawing by Thomas Theodor Heine,
see Note on page viii

ARK

FRANK KERMODE
ROMANTIC IMAGE

ARK PAPERBACKS

First published in 1957
ARK Edition 1986
ARK PAPERBACKS is an imprint of

Routledge & Kegan Paul plc

11 New Fetter Lane, London EC4P 4EE, England

Published in the USA by
Routledge & Kegan Paul Inc.
in association with Methuen Inc.
29 West 35th Street, New York, NY 1001

Printed in Great Britain
by Cox & Wyman Ltd., Reading

ISBN 0 7448 0037 4

If the Spectator could enter into these Images in his Imagination, approaching them on the Fiery Chariot of his Contemplative Thought. . . or could make a Friend & Companion of one of these Images of wonder. . . then would he arise from his Grave, then would he meet the Lord in the Air & then he would be happy.

Here they are no longer talking of what is Good & Evil, or of what is Right or Wrong, & puzzling themselves in Satan's Labyrinth, But are Conversing with Eternal Realities as they Exist in the Human Imagination. We are in a World of Generation & death & this world we must cast off if we would be Painters such as Rafael, Mich. Angelo & the Ancient Sculptors.

BLAKE

He has made, after the manner of his kind,
Mere images.   YEATS

PREFACE

I have written this essay because I thought I could see a new way of looking at certain assumptions which are of great importance to contemporary poetry and criticism. Very briefly, these assumptions are that the image is, in Wyndham Lewis's phrase, the 'primary pigment' of poetry; and that the poet who uses it is by that very fact differentiated from other men, and seriously at odds with the society in which he has to live. Thoroughly Romantic they may be, but they are none the less fundamental to much twentieth-century thinking about poetry; and this remains true for critics and poets who are militantly anti-Romantic.

Clearly this is a complicated subject, and equally clearly my essay is short and tentative, laying no claim to exhaustive or specialist scholarship. Everybody agrees that dons are deplorably specialised these days, and this is not, as they say, my 'period'. But I have not thrown caution to the winds, and I have accepted scholarly assistance wherever I could get it. (I say this, of course, without prejudice to my benefactors.) I am particularly indebted to Professor Mario Praz's *The Romantic Agony* (Oxford, 1933); to M. Albert Béguin's *L'Ame romantique et le rêve* (2nd. ed., Paris, 1946); to Professor A. G. Lehmann's *The Symbolist Aesthetic in France* (Oxford, 1950); and to Professor M. H. Abrams' *The Mirror and the Lamp* (Oxford, 1953).

I have also had the benefit of conversation with Professor Lehmann, and particularly with Mr. Iain Fletcher, who most generously shared his knowledge of the poets of the 1890s, and read the essay in an early version. Professor D. J. Gordon read a later draft, and made valuable suggestions for its improvement. These acknowledgments do not exhaust my indebtedness to other books and friends. I mention only those obligations which it woud be scandalous not to confess.

Thanks are due to the following for their kind permission to use copyright material: Mrs W. B. Yeats, Messrs MacMillan and Co., the Editor of *The Observer*, and Herr Erich Seemann.

F. K.

A NOTE ON THE FRONTISPIECE

Thomas Theodor Heine (1867–1948), caricaturist and illustrator, was one of the founders of the famous periodical *Simplicissimus* in 1896. Dancers were favourite subjects of his, and his treatment of them shows to a marked degree the influence of Beardsley. This drawing of Loïe Fuller appeared in a periodical called *Die Insel*, founded in 1899 and published by Schuster and Loeffler in Berlin: Dr. Leopold Ettlinger, to whom I am indebted for this information, calls it 'a real *art nouveau* period piece'. Loïe Fuller was valued not only by devotees of *art nouveau* for the exotic naturalism of her dancing, but by Symbolists as the finest example of the use of the dance as an emblem of the Image of art. This drawing is the best visual illustration I could discover – better, I think, than Toulouse-Lautrec's 'Loïe Fuller' – for Chapter 4 of this book. Mallarmé's comments on Loïe Fuller will be found on pages 71 and 72.

CONTENTS

PREFACE   VII

A NOTE ON THE FRONTISPIECE   VIII

PART ONE: DANCER AND TREE

   I. THE ARTIST IN ISOLATION   1
  II. 'IN MEMORY OF MAJOR ROBERT GREGORY'   30
 III. THE IMAGE   43
  IV. THE DANCER   49
   V. THE TREE   92

PART TWO: THE TWENTIETH CENTURY

  VI. ARTHUR SYMONS   107
 VII. T. E. HULME   119
 VIII. 'DISSOCIATION OF SENSIBILITY'   138
  IX. CONCLUSION   162

INDEX   167

PART ONE

DANCER AND TREE

.

How can we know the dancer from the dance?
YEATS

I
THE ARTIST IN ISOLATION

Je ne suis pas fait comme aucun de ceux que j'ai
sus. Mais si je ne vaux pas mieux, au moins je suis
autre.

ROUSSEAU

We poets in our youth begin in gladness,
But thereof comes in the end despondency and
madness

WORDSWORTH

As its title is intended to indicate, this essay is primarily
concerned with the evolution of assumptions relating
to the image of poetry; it is an attempt to describe this
image in a new way, and to suggest new ways of looking at
contingent issues, in poetry and criticism. The main topic is, in
fact, that 'esthetic image' explained in Thomist language by
Stephen Dedalus in the *Portrait of the Artist as a Young Man*: it is
for him that beauty which has the three attributes of integrity,
consonance and clarity; which is "apprehended as one thing...
self-bounded and self-contained upon the immeasurable background of space or time which is not it"; apprehended in its
quidditas by the artist whose mind is arrested in "a luminous
stasis of esthetic pleasure".

This is only one famous — and rather obscure — way of
putting it, and the conclusions concerning poetry at which
Joyce, starting from this position, arrives, are characteristic of
the whole movement I shall discuss. One such conclusion is
that the artist who is vouchsafed this power of apprehending

1

the Image — to experience that 'epiphany' which is the Joycean equivalent of Pater's 'vision' — has to pay a heavy price in suffering, to risk his immortal soul, and to be alone, "not only to be separate from all others but to have not even one friend".

These two beliefs — in the Image as a radiant truth out of space and time, and in the necessary isolation or estrangement of men who can perceive it — are inextricably associated, and because of their interdependence I find that I must begin this essay on the Image with a few pages on what is for me the subsidiary theme, this ubiquitous assumption that the artist is cut off from other men; and even these notes will contain some anticipations of later chapters on the Image proper.

The author to whom it would be natural to turn for a fully developed view of both themes is Thomas Mann, who sets them, so to speak, in the full context of modern life and learning. They occur in singular and suggestive purity — if that is the word — in the early stories *Death in Venice* and *Tonio Kröger*, and later receive encyclopaedic enlargement. The first of these stories is nevertheless the most systematic exposition, in art, that I have so far encountered. But for my purposes the topic of isolation is more directly relevant as it occurs in poetry, and more particularly in English poetry, since what I have to say later about Yeats is the heart of this essay. The real difficulty about this topic is to know where to start; the literature of the past hundred and fifty years has millions of texts for discourses upon it, and in any case the 'difference' of artists is common ground to the artists themselves and to those who hate them. Perhaps we need an exhaustive study in critical, psychological, and sociological terms; that would be a daunting task, involving the history of the very tools one was using. All I intend here is to recall to mind a few aspects of the subject which seem indispensable to what I have to say about the Image.

Occasionally one encounters the paradox that the artist is magnificently sane, only the quality of his sanity distinguishing him from other men. His *sensibility* (in Henry James's sense, the 'very atmosphere of his mind') is more profound, subtle and receptive, and his powers of organizing experience very much greater. His art is not made of stuff inaccessible to them; there is no qualitative difference between his way of knowing

2

and theirs; all depends upon this intensity of organization. Pater said it in his liturgical monotone; Dr. Richards said it in his scientific parables, making the point with the aid of diagrams. (These critics, saying the same thing in their so different ways, span a period in which many voices, proclaiming novelty, seem on analysis to be saying much the same thing.) But Pater also knew the cost of this intensity; the Cyrenaic visions, "almost beatific", of ideal personalities in life and art were "a very costly matter," requiring "the sacrifice of a thousand possible sympathies" and so effectively setting the visionary apart. And this is characteristic of the way in which the paradox of the artist's 'normality' melts away into the received opinion: artists are different, isolated.

It is important to distinguish, in passing, between this opinion as a serious belief held by and about artists, and the vulgarized bohemian tradition that the artist is poor, immoral, and marked by an eccentricity of costume. This is really a confused echo from the Paris of Mürger and Huysmans and the *poètes maudits*, with a few collateral English rumours. As an example (rather a sophisticated one, indeed) of the persistence of the lowbrow version, here is a passage from a notice in a London evening paper of an exhibition of paintings by M. Bernard Buffet (1955):

Three years ago you could have bought a Buffet for the cost of a meal but now the Buffet price is £300-£500. He has just been voted France's leading young painter in a ballot run by a glossy art magazine. . . which says one of the causes of his success is that he painted the miseries of youth after the war. Only 27 now, he was 18 when the critics first acclaimed him. At the time he was living the real, un-glamorised Bohemian life, going without food to buy canvas. . . He works entirely from memory and imagination, and by electric light. The house he has had built in the Basses Alpes is specially designed to exclude the beautiful views that other people would dote upon. Nothing must disturb his imagination.

An accompanying reproduction of a painting by M. Buffet shows that he takes his isolation as his subject. What is expected to appeal to the public is the 'human interest' of such eccentricity. Why build the house there, amid the 'beautiful views' (it is 'natural' and decent to admire the view, and normal painters, not these modern madmen, would be outside with an easel) if you are going to work out of your own head? 'Imagination' is what M. Buffet works by; but "it's all imagination" can mean different things to different people, and the meaning the public is here expected to supply is that which places 'imagination' in an antithetical relationship with 'reality'. The philistines, though they were long ago bludgeoned into accepting 'nature' as a mysteriously good thing, cannot see M. Buffet's work as anything but fantastic nonsense, whereas for him their 'nature' is dead, and the concern only of a science which specialized in measuring dead things. He is interested in what he has access to, and they have not — the image that is truth *because* he makes it up; *because* it has nothing to do with 'nature'. There was once a *New Yorker* joke about a haggard genius who said "I paint what I *don't* see". This joke, good as it is, depends on our readiness to think of 'modern art' as fantastic nonsense, and the drawing has to show a Simeon Solomon type, garret-dwelling, ragged, pitiable but also odious; for nearly two centuries there have been painters who would not have seen this joke (except by some special effort of sympathy) because the old scarecrow is saying something that has, for them, a great deal of truth in it. For them, and for M. Buffet, these public misunderstandings are merely another aspect of their isolation. For we may roughly distinguish two aspects of the condition. The first is represented by M. Buffet's voluntary, even somewhat ostentatious, retreat to the Alps, his blocking the windows to keep out the normally beautiful views and the normally welcomed daylight; this is the cult of isolated joy, the pursuit of the Image by the specially fated and highly organized artist, a man who gets things out of his own head. He excludes society and its half-baked sensibilities. The second is the reaction of astonishment and contempt in those who 'dote upon' beautiful views. Whether he likes it or not, society excludes him.

Each of these aspects is in turn presented (though of course not in this very simple way) as the whole truth about the estrangement of the modern artist, though the second is the more popular. Of course they are really inseparable. The artist's devotion to the Image developed at the same time as the modern industrial state and the modern middle class. From the beginnings of Romantic poetry the artist has been, as M. Béguin says of Lichtenberg, "malade de sa différence avec son temps". The great poet of the modern city, Baudelaire, was a self-confessed 'seer'. The *frisson nouveau* upon which Hugo congratulated him proceeded from the study of a fallen humanity in the new context; his mythology is of the perversion, the *ennui*, the metaphysical despair of men and women subjected to what Dickens (in this respect Baudelaire's English equivalent — compare *Le crépuscule du matin* with certain passages in *Little Dorrit*) called "the shame, desertion, wretchedness and exposure of the great capital". The poet, though devoted to the Image, belongs to this city, his place in which Baudelaire notoriously compares with that of the prostitute. All men, he says, have an "invincible taste for prostitution", and he calls this the source of man's "horror of solitude"; the poet is different in that he wants to be alone, but this is only "prostituting yourself in a special way"; as Mr. Turnell says in his recent book on Baudelaire, this attempt at unity in solitude fails because of internal stress and division, and the poet can claim not unity but only difference in the manner of his prostitution. Yet Baudelaire, so sensitive to the horror of the modern city, remains true to a central Romantic tradition in abstaining from any attempt to alter the social order, and despises the "puerile Utopias" of some other Romantic poets. And his answer to the question, what has the movement, whose poets find themselves in this dreadful situation, done for us, is striking: it has "recalled us to the truth of the image". The Image is the reward of that agonising difference; isolated in the city, the poet is a 'seer'. The Image, for all its concretion, precision, and oneness, is desperately difficult to communicate, and has for that reason alone as much to do with the alienation of the seer as the necessity of his existing in the midst of a hostile society.

Baudelaire is a famous case, but there is nothing specifically French about his difficulties, and these notions of Image and isolation developed independently in England, from native Romantic roots. The Symbol of the French is, as we shall see, the Romantic Image writ large and given more elaborate metaphysical and magical support; and, if we go back far enough, we can see that English poets — using the same ultimate sources, Boehme and Swedenborg, the Germans of the later eighteenth century — developed their own way of "recalling us to the truth of the image". This native tradition is in some ways more significant for modern poetry than imported

Symbolism; Blake and Pater stand behind Yeats at his most magnificent, and in the thought of Arthur Symons, crucial for the historian, they are at least as important as the French poets. And an awareness of the Image involves, for English poets also, a sense of powerful forces extruding them from the life of their society, a sense of irreconcileable difference and precarious communication. Here too we encounter that ambiguity concerning the degree of responsibility for the poet's estrangement. Obviously it is too simple to say, with the prose Arnold and with Mencken, each criticising the materialism of his own society, that the artist is forced into seclusion; that is where, on his own view, he has to be. The ambiguity is very acutely presented by D. H. Lawrence (who certainly earned the right to understand it) in a comment on Beethoven's letters: "always in love with somebody when he wasn't really, and wanting contacts when he didn't really — part of the crucifixion into isolate individuality — *poveri noi*". The crux of the matter is in this colloquial 'really'; did he or didn't he want such contacts, was he natural man or artist, did he want to 'go out of himself' or not? 'Crucifixion' (a word that recurs with significant frequency in this context, from Kierkegaard to Yeats and Wilde) does not completely exclude the idea of torment freely though painfully chosen; *poveri noi*, however you look at it we artists are all in the same boat, whether we 'really' like it or not. To be cut off from life and action, in one way or another, is necessary as a preparation for the 'vision'. Some difference in the artist gives him access to this — an enormous privilege, involving *joy* (which acquires an almost technical sense as a necessary concomitant of the full exercise of the mind in the act of imagination). But the power of joy being possible only to a profound 'organic sensibility', a man who experiences it will also suffer exceptionally. He must be lonely, haunted, victimised, devoted to suffering rather than action — or, to state this in a manner more acceptable to the twentieth century, he is exempt from the normal human orientation towards action and so enabled to intuit those images which are truth, in defiance of the triumphant claims of merely intellectual disciplines. But that is pushing too far ahead. I have now introduced into the discussion the crucial concept of *joy*, of which the *locus classicus* is Coleridge's Ode; and I now turn more specifically to the English tradition.

6

The 'difference' of some of the English Romantic poets is almost too well known; they were outcast because they had to pay for their joy and their vision. Sometimes they attributed their condition to some malady in themselves, but they also blamed the age in which they lived, as Hazlitt did when he measured the sad alteration of the world by comparing the art of West with that of Raphael, in which "every nerve and muscle has intense feeling". How often are we to hear this repeated! For Yeats the painters to be compared are Sargent and Titian. The alienation of the artist and this despair at the decay of the world are two sides of one coin; the present age is the one that hates art, some earlier age loved the poet without corrupting him. So it was that Hazlitt found in Godwin's *St. Leon* a magician who could stand for the modern artist, and who might just as easily have come from some fantasy after Villiers de l'Isle Adam:

> He is a limb torn off from society. In possession of eternal youth and beauty he can feel no love; surrounded, tantalized and tormented by riches, he can do no good. The faces of men pass before him as in a speculum; but he is attached to them by no common tie of sympathy or suffering. He is thrown back into himself and his own thoughts. He lives in the solitude of his own breast, without wife or child or friend or enemy in the whole world. His is the solitude of the soul, not of woods or trees or mountains — but the desert of society — the waste and oblivion of the heart. He is himself alone.

Keats will show us how this kind of thing gets into poetry. He gave his full and considered approval to these passionate remarks of Hazlitt, and himself undertook to "live like a hermit" in the midst of the world, and "bear anything — any misery, even imprisonment — so long as I have neither wife nor child". He even thanked the "English world" for its cruelty to writers, saying that it "ill-treated them during their lives and fostered them after their deaths" so that "they have in general been trampled aside into the bye paths of life and seen the festerings of Society"; yet this is "one of the great reasons that the English have produced the finest writers in the world". Keats very naturally related the artist's joy to his suffering:

Ay, in the very temple of Delight
Veil'd Melancholy has her sovran shrine,
Though seen of none save him whose strenuous tongue
Can burst Joy's grape against his palate fine;
His soul shall taste the sadness of her might,
And be among her cloudy trophies hung.

This view of melancholy-in-genius probably goes back, through Burton, to an older opinion of the necessity of melancholy in artists: we have a sudden perspective, back to Dürer and Ficino. But it looks forward also, for here, very richly and completely, is the artist as a man of high 'sensibility' — *feeling* with remarkable intensity as a necessity of genius; and here too is the artist as victim, that other necessary consequence. Keats, indeed, seems to me to have been the first to achieve in English a characteristic poetic statement of the joy and cost of the Image — his is more central, I think, than Shelley's somewhat similar efforts, more imitable than Coleridge's. I am thinking not of *Lamia* (where the tension is between the luxurious and decorative but still sinister, chthonic, image of poetry, and 'cold philosophy') but to *Hyperion*, and particularly to the second draft. That version begins with the poet's claim to a higher dream than the mere fanatic's. He tells his vision: in a sort of earthly paradise he drank from an enchanted vessel, and this set him apart from other men, like the touch of the Sidhe in Celtic mythology. He falls into a sleep within his dream, and awakes in a sanctuary; with terror and anguish he approaches an altar from which issues a voice promising him, as a reward, a mitigation of mortality. He has, says the voice, "felt What 'tis to die and live again before Thy fated hour"; though some fail in the ascent to the altar, and "Rot on the pavement where thou rottedst half". Unlike the normal man, who knows joy and pain "alone, distinct", the poet "venoms all his days, Bearing more woes than all his sins deserve". It is to soften this fate that he is admitted to the sanctuary and its altar. A cut passage in the manuscript, which shows us how Keats's mind was working, describes how the poet distinguishes himself from mock-artists. He asks where he is, before whose altar he stands. It is the altar of Moneta, sole divine survivor of the Saturnian age, Goddess of Memory and Mother of the Muses. Moneta, I take it, represents the survival of the archaic way of thought — imaginative rather than discursive ("the large utterance of the early gods''), *un-dissociated*, mythopoeic; more profound, though certainly, to use the word in a limiting sense, less *human* than the discourse of 'philosophy' which Keats, with his tentative evolutionism, was trying to accept as a necessary human development. This is the philosophy that explicates the rainbow in terms of the spectrum, but it also promises a diminution of human misery; the Lamia of poetry shrivels before it, but Apollonius is after all only being considerate. Moneta is a painful survival, in a world that has, in its 'philosophic' way, disentangled the dream of imagination from true knowledge. Her children are the patronesses of the arts that preserve, in this hostile later world, the old intuitive knowing that men admired and associated with the angels. It is access to the knowledge she represents that distinguishes the poet; and this poet is permitted to see her face, which is described in a very remarkable passage:

> Then saw I a wan face,
> Not pined by human sorrows, but bright-blanch'd
> By an immortal sickness which kills not;
> It works a constant change, which happy death
> Can put no end to; deathwards progressing
> To no death was the visage; it had past
> The lily and the snow; and beyond these
> I must not think now, though I saw that face.
> But for her eyes I should have fled away;
> They held me back with a benignant light,
> Soft, mitigated by divinest lids
> Half-closed, and visionless entire they seem'd
> Of all external things; they saw me not,
> But in blank splendour beam'd, like the mild moon,
> Who comforts those she sees not, who knows not
> What eyes are upward cast.

Moneta is full of terrible knowledge, and this knowledge is about to be revealed to the poet; it is the myth of the Titans, and for Keats myth was of the same imaginative order as the poet's knowledge. She is immortal; her face is the emblem of the cost as well as of the benefits of knowledge and immortality. Moneta's face haunts many later poets as well as Keats. It has the pallor and the equivocal life-in-death of Coleridge's spectre — whiter in disease than the hands of Venus and Adonis, which, after the *Biographia Literaria*, were strongly associated with the act of imagination. The face is alive only in a chill and inhuman way. The knowledge it represents is not malign, but it is unrelated to 'external things'; the eyes express nothing, looking inward to the "high tragedy In the dark secret chambers of the skull". To prostrate himself before this figure is the privilege of the artist's joy and the reward of his suffering. The face of Moneta is an emblem we shall often encounter again in these pages.

The other version of *Hyperion* has yet more of this association of suffering and joy, in the account of the apotheosis of Apollo. But indeed this association is at the root of Romantic thought.

> Joy is the sweet voice, Joy the luminous cloud –
>   We in ourselves rejoice!
> And thence flows all that charms or ear or sight,
>   All melodies the echo of that voice,
>   All colours a suffusion of that light.

And Joy cannot be had without anguish. Wordsworth's poet is a "man speaking to men", dealing with "Joy in widest commonalty spread". But already in the Preface of 1800 he allows a difference between poets and other men, though insisting that it is only a difference of degree; this was forced on him by his belief in the uniformity of human personality, which also bred the theory of diction (the language of poets comes not from poets but from men). Yet Wordsworth's belief that the poet is more highly organised, more passionate and subtle, than the peasant, in fact puts as much distance between poet and peasant as between peasant and amoeba. Already the poet is necessarily estranged, and his work may become increasingly unintelligible and offensive to all who cannot share his dream and his persecution, or believe that the grounds of his joy are true.

> What portion in the world can the artist have
> That has awakened from the common dream,
> But dissipation and despair?

This is Yeats, more categorical than Wordsworth. Yet Wordsworth had to admit (thinking of Burns) that the artist's peculiar susceptibility to pleasure made him an easy victim of vicious temptations, and therefore a man especially prone to misery. He feels more pleasure, but also more pain. His difference isolates him; he incurs hatred for all sorts of reasons — for his sinewy thigh, for his claim of agonised privilege; but there is little he can do save to trust in the Image, to weld joy and misery together in some symbolic blaze, some 'Leech Gatherer'; and, that victory over, plan another. "Among subjective men," says Yeats, "the victory is an intellectual daily recreation of all that exterior fate snatches away, and so that fate's antithesis. We begin to live when we have conceived life as a tragedy." But even tragedy is a matter of joy; Hamlet and Lear are gay. Wordsworth was always aware of this. All his great solitaries are tragic figures, and he had an extraordinary relish for the appearances of disaster and misery. Leaving the Ruined Cottage, the poet "walks along his road in happiness"; in the drowned man taken from the lake, a "spectre shape of terror", he finds, imagination aiding, "a dignity, a smoothness, like the works of Grecian art". In what is perhaps the most tremendous passage in *The Prelude* he demonstrates the conversion of a 'visionary dreariness' — the "naked pool",

> The beacon crowning the lone eminence,
> The female with her garments vexed and tossed
> By the strong wind –

by the 'spirit of pleasure' into profound joy. It is one of Yeats's 'victories'. What saves the poet here is the symbol-making power; it is not what the Leech Gatherer says, but the fact that Wordsworth could invent him, that saves his joy and his sanity, gives him his victory. But of course there is always a last victory; and that is the Romantic poet's Dejection Ode, which exhausts him.

I dwell on this rather grim emphasis on pleasure (which, as Coleridge and Arnold also believed, must be felt before it can be communicated) because it is vital to the conception of the isolated poet. *Joy* is what they have to communicate, and it is good. They are in no position to teach, and indeed have a great dread of the didactic; but they have redefined the relationship of *utile* to *dulce*, and usually believe in their moral function, so that, in short, the pleasure communicated conduces to morality. That is why George Eliot, in some ways a typical Romantic artist, could call herself an 'aesthetic teacher', and yet protest that she had no desire to instruct or change the world; that is why, to our great benefit, Pater in *The Renaissance* and *Marius*

11

the Epicurean, and James in 'The Art of Fiction' and in his practice, insisted upon the moral value of what is highly organised and profoundly apprehended, in life and in art.

The position is, of course, easily misunderstood, particularly when expressed by such formulae as "All art is quite useless". "The artist must serve Mammon," said Keats; this makes it easy to behave like an artist. We have no space to treat of frauds and misconceptions; but it remains true that corruption in an artist (a condition perhaps not fully described before Collingwood's *Principles of Art*) came to be regarded as another matter from corruption in another man. His purity cannot be judged by the rough standards that serve in the world; it is primarily an aesthetic purity. Here we have a situation for Jamesian comedy perhaps; at any rate, it can be made to seem serious in one way or another by a James or a Yeats or a Mann. (Yeats said he had seen more artists ruined by wives and children than by harlots.) Yet a whole gifted generation of English poets which held these views in an extreme form, and which Yeats calls a 'tragic generation' never seem to be taken seriously at all. The reason is, partly, that in such extreme formulations as Wilde's, the doctrine is unpalatable; but it is also, partly, that these poets have come to be regarded as exotics, outside the main English tradition. Since this is an important generation of poets for my purposes, I must try briefly to remedy this by dwelling for a moment on Arnold and Pater, and particularly on Arnold.

Arnold was a very influential transmitter of Romantic thought, and no one was more fully aware of our problem, under all its aspects, than he. Unhappily, he himself rejected *Empedocles on Etna*, in this connexion his most important poem; and consequently it is not much read. If it were, we should be less prone to think of the poets of the nineties as merely wayward young men who picked up bad habits from the French.

Arnold's attitude to this poem — in some ways a great poem, profound and finely-designed — is exasperating. We might paraphrase Blake's remark on Wordsworth's criticism, and say of the 1853 *Preface*, "I do not know who wrote this Preface; it is very mischievous, and directly contrary to Arnold's own practice". It was written by Arnold's spectre. Or perhaps we should say that the rejection was the work of Arnold the Critic, who rightly distrusted poems which were victories to Arnold the poet, but messages of despair to one who saw the need to get poetry usefully working, leavening the lump. Indeed, his turning away from the poem is in a sense a personal consequence of the suicide of Empedocles; the poem wrote off Arnold's main topic. It contains his solution — Empedocles is Arnold's Leech Gatherer. But there seemed no prospect of indefinitely repeating this victory (Pyrrhic, because suicide is the least useful of answers in *life*) and so Arnold rejects it in favour of another solution which involves not death but merely poetic extinction, or rather a curiously effective compromise which keeps the poet in a state of suspended animation. At any rate there is no need to accept the dismissal of a poem by its author simply because it happened not to be the kind of poem he liked after he had finished it (though, with his oddly literal acceptance of the Romantic pleasure-principle, Arnold thought his own enjoyment a certain index of other people's).

The gist of his complaint in the Preface — that dry attempt to direct poetry back to its 'normal' material, the unchanging human heart — is that in *Empedocles* suffering finds no vent in action, everything is to be endured and nothing to be done. But in fact the poem, designed with extraordinary care, a professional job of architectonics, is a system of tensions which deliberately excludes all movement save the suicide of the hero. Empedocles is the Romantic poet who knows enough; Callicles the Romantic poet who does not know enough. "Wordsworth's sweet calm" is no longer available; it is Sénancour who knows the situation through and through; *Eternité, deviens mon asile!* is his admired epitaph, and Empedocles' "Receive me, save me!" is the same thing. *Greater by far that thou art dead.*

> Ah! two desires toss about
> The poet's feverish blood.
> One drives him to the world without,
>   And one to solitude.

Obermann deals with the privileged moments of the poet driven into solitude, moments when the truth is known to be interior, independent of sensible reality or perceived in that reality by a mystical intuition; there is a momentary euphoria, joy, in this participation of the mind with the perceived harmonious order, which has to be paid for. (Incidentally, the

13

thought of Sénancour, like that of Novalis, Blake, Coleridge and later Romantics, stems in part from the hermetic thought of the sixteenth and seventeenth centuries; the movement, like Kierkegaard's poet, was unhappily in love with God.) Arnold augmented the profound insight into isolation which Sénancour provided, by his reading in Maurice de Guérin, a poet who knew "the freshness of the early world" and was tortured by the rarity and brevity of those moments of imaginative perception he was always seeking to recapture. For him it was the imagination that made truth; "rarement on a fait, autant que lui," says M. Béguin, "confiance à l'efficacité des images; le mot imagination était pour lui 'le nom de la vie intérieure' ". But as a direct consequence of such searching and such confidence in the interior life, he believed that the poet will always be pursued from exile to exile, with no continuing stay; and he meditated upon the permanent and luxurious escape of death. From such sources derives the figure of the Romantic poet which, in his play, Arnold dissociates, so to speak, into the persons of Empedocles and Callicles.

Of course he himself was such a poet; but he had some confidence that the intolerable situation of himself and his like would end when (hastened by Criticism) a new social order would make poetry possible, and a "joy whose grounds are true"; and Sénancour, from his grave, counsels the ageing Arnold to continue the task of Criticism:

> But thou, though to the world's new hour
> Thou come with aspect marr'd,
> Shorn of the joy, the bloom, the power,
> Which best befits its bard –

> ...Though late, though dimm'd, though weak, yet tell
> Hope to a world new-made!

Empedocles abandons contemplation, acts and dies; Arnold acts and lives, as a critic, a disengaged, antididactic critic; still seeing widely and steadily, but talking of society, not so much of the poet in society, seeking to end rather than to analyse that problem by the reform of society; dealing, at any rate, in life, not in art, becoming not being.

But *Empedocles* is about art, or rather about the artist. It is a victory fought over the same ground as 'The Strayed Reveller'.

Empedocles belonged to a great age of poetry, an age of acceptable *Aberglaube*, an age when the poet had a function (specified as therapeutic) in society. But the new age excludes him, or rather he excludes himself from a new society,

> since this new swarm
> Of sophists has got empire in our schools
> Where he was paramount, since he is banish'd
> And lives a lonely man in triple gloom.

To the young Callicles there is nothing genuine in the plight of Empedocles. Callicles has not yet understood. "The sophists are no enemies of his," he says, and prefers what is for himself the more comfortable explanation, that Empedocles has "some root of suffering in himself". More comfortable, but not false; what Callicles does not yet know — it is the first of many ironies in the structure of the work — is that he too must have this 'root of suffering'. At present, his "tongue outruns his knowledge". He is sent to the lower slope. Callicles has already progressed some way — he has abandoned the sensual feast below; but he has no place as yet on the top of the mountain, the eminence of isolation and self-destruction.

There follows a richly ironical debate between a poet ignorant enough to know joy and an ex-poet who knows that its grounds are not true, who scrabbles prosaically among the rubbish for the ethical fragments of which he must try to build himself a shelter. The great risk Arnold had to take here was, technically, analogous to putting a bore in a play; he may be boring. Arnold's extinct poet has to be flat and joyless; the solution is to make him sing like a tired Browning, and it is perhaps not a good solution. But the failure is not complete, though a line-by-line analysis might suggest that it is. The 'poetry', spontaneous, local, charming, 'Keatsian', as natural as the leaves on the tree, but fundamentally inept and doomed, flows from the younger poet, who is still in love with his dream, still unaware of its falsity and uselessness, and of the cost of his art; still unbroken by its rigours. Callicles sings the heroic wisdom of Chiron and Peleus; Empedocles replies with a long poem advocating a sober epicureanism which, with traditional anti-intellectualism (different in orientation, it should be noted, from the genuine Romantic variety found in Wordsworth and Coleridge, Rossetti, Pater, Wilde and Yeats) calls the village churl nearer the truth than the poet, with his "estranged eyes". The answering song of Callicles is one of Arnold's most perfect poems, and this not merely in its rich and delicate texture, but in the precision of its structural ironies. He extracts a Wordsworthian joy — the rejected joy — from the tragedy of Cadmus and Harmonia, confidently asserting that happy immortality of the tormented soul which is the lie hidden in the joy. Empedocles, for all his knowledge and experience, cannot resist it; "How his brow lightened as the music rose!" But this is Arnold's act-ending; and immediately the ironies become more conclusive, the situation more explicit.

> No, thou art come too late, Empedocles,
> And the world hath the day, and must break thee,
> Not thou the world. With men thou canst not live,
> Their thoughts, their ways, their wishes, are not thine;
> And being lonely thou art miserable,
> For something has impaired thy spirit's strength,
> And dried its self-sufficing fount of joy,
> Thou canst not live with men or with thyself –
> O sage! O sage! – Take then the one way left; . . .
> Before the soul lose all her solemn joys,
> And awe be dead, and hope impossible,
> And the soul's deep eternal night come on,
> Receive me, hide me, quench me, take me home!

But as he advances to the crater's edge, the voice of Callicles floats up, bearing another lovely fable that mythologizes the mountain's destructive power; he is content with the beauty of the Titan's anguish, and does not comment upon it; it is not for him to draw conclusions. His pleasure is the same, whether he is considering the sufferings of Typho or the "awful pleasure bland" of Jove, and his unspeakable content under the ministrations of Hebe, whose "flush'd feet glow on the marble floor". The joy of Callicles turns it all to joy. But Empedocles allegorizes the poet's myth:

> He fables, yet speaks truth!
> The brave, impetuous heart yields everywhere
> To the subtle contriving head;
> Great qualities are trodden down,
> And littleness united
> To become invincible.

16

"Great art beaten down. . . the best lack all conviction. . ." All that has happened, on this view, between Arnold and Yeats, is that the wicked have discovered the lost intensity of the good; the world has become, as no one could foresee, more murderous as well as darker. At this latest outburst of false joy, Empedocles resigns the symbols of his wisdom; at the next he lays aside his laurel bough. The song of Callicles is the beautiful and ironical song of the flaying of Marsyas at the orders of the cold and beautiful god — Marsyas, the first victim of that presumptuous devotion. (Pater thought of Raphael's 'Apollo and Marsyas' almost as "a parable of the contention between classic art and the romantic"; and it is possible that Arnold felt something of this also, making his god cold and marmoreal, without Dionysiac elements.) Empedocles is the god's latest victim:

> And lie thou there,
> My laurel bough!. . .
> I am weary of thee,
> I am weary of the solitude
> Which he who bears thee must abide –
> Of the rocks of Parnassus,
> Of the rocks of Delphi,
> Of the moonlit peaks and the caves.
> Thou guardest them, Apollo!
> Over the grave of the slain Pytho.
> Though young, intolerably severe!
> Thou keepest aloof the profane,
> But the solitude oppresses thy votary!

Cut off from the profane, he is cut off from life, to which he is instinctively propelled; but life is what he cannot live, and he flies from it to intolerable solitude:

> only death
> Can cut his oscillations short, and so
> Bring him to poise.

A certain action, a violent process of life, is possible to the contemplative and to the artist; but the cost is extinction. What cannot be had is the slow economical burning away of life; the damp faggots. Callicles, lower down, does not know this. When young

> we received the shock of mighty thoughts
> On simple minds with a pure natural joy;

17

but, this stage past, life is "ceaseless opposition", living a doomed attempt to preserve the "dwindling faculty of joy". Thinking of the sweet singing Callicles, the sage adds:

> Joy and the outward world must die to him
> As they are dead to me.

Callicles is given the last word. He is still far from the necessity of saving himself by fire; the outward world and the inward dream are still consistent, orderly and beautiful. Poetry
belongs to this apparent joy, not to the truth of disaster:

> Not here, O Apollo!
> Are haunts meet for thee
> But Callicles will learn.

To describe the drama in these terms is like saying that the
point of "Resolution and Independance" is:

> I could have laughed myself to scorn to find
> In that decrepit man so firm a mind.

The *rightness* of Callicles is not in question, nor is that of
Empedocles; the poem does not offer that kind of answer
(what good poem, the tradition has taught us to say, would?)
What Callicles says is 'wrong', but only by a false abstraction,
for his words are part of a larger organization of words and
images (in the sense of the word discussed later in this book)
and their discursive truth or falsity is simply not the point. The
poem is a victory; or, in another legitimate formula, a momentary stasis in an endless process, keeping a marble or a bronze
repose. The question for the poet, however, is, where is the
next victory to come from? Must he always write to end isolation for a moment? Arnold found this solution intolerable,
suppressed *Empedocles* because it had no action, and set out to
reform the world that was culpable of this absurd situation;
forgetting perhaps, that "root of suffering". He plunged into
action, into other people's business; we may remember Yeats's
self-criticism: "every enterprise that offered, allured just so far
as it was not my business", and the colder self-censure: "I had
surrendered to the chief temptation of the artist, creation without toil". For in so far as Arnold was an artist — and he surely
was a very considerable one — the answer to his dilemma, in

18

the terms in which he undoubtedly understood it, lay in the cruel effort and continued self-expenditure of a series of Empedoclean victories, not in the carefully qualified betrayal, the compromise of life and art, action and inaction, which his Mask as Critic represents.

To himself, or to his notebook, Arnold would obviously not put it in this way (and of course, in any case, I boldly simplify). Arnold knew all about masks, and he knew about the Image, and what it costs; he abandoned it not only because it seemed to lack utility, but to save his soul. This may seem a dramatic way of putting it, yet not only Yeats but Pope would have understood it. Inert melancholy means self-destruction; hence all the exhortations to *Tüchtigkeit*, the repeated admonitions of the Notebooks: *Ecce labora et noli contristari*. Be known in action, not in suffering; seek light and not shade. Sénancour was seductive, but Sainte-Beuve was sane, and had little time for *poètes maudits*. Perhaps Arnold did alter his world, perhaps he even made it a little more like his dream. At any rate, he acted, and he got out of poetry and the dreadful fate of Empedocles. There is a sharp contrast here with Yeats, who, equally aware of the proble,m and seeing it in very similar terms, knew why he wanted the management of men, understood his own guilt and felt conscious of damnation; he did not walk out of his dream, but simply extended it to include everything, and went on being a poet till he died.

It may seem curious that Arnold rather than Pater, who was much less reservedly admired in the 'nineties, should be the writer who most completely states the nineteenth-century English version of the old problem, how is the artist different, and what is the nature of his special access to truth, provided he has one; but Arnold was steeped in Romantic literature in three languages, and it is the dominance of the critic-school-inspector that precludes our seeing him in the first place as a fully Romantic, though fully critical, poet. Like his contemporaries on the Continent, though in different terms, he was disposed to see the prophetic or rhapsodic element in the poet as antithetical to the cast of mind which succeeded in 'science'; but, unlike them, he so far accepted the valuation of scientists as to be content with the identification of poetry and that *Aberglaube* of which scientific criticism was depriving religion.

This solution did not recommend itself to later English poets in the tradition; but they were, I think, aware of the importance of Arnold's grasp of the problem, and his influence upon them was more considerable and direct than might easily be believed.

It is nevertheless true that Pater, though equally preoccupied with the problem of incorporating the *utile* into the *dulce*, found answers which were at once more congenial to artists who wanted to go on being artists, and more liable to debasement. Perhaps in his life Pater exhibits, though in a manner peculiar to himself, the stigmata of isolation: without risking the uncharted portions of his biography we can at least remind ourselves of the famous and curious visit to London, immediately after the publication of *Marius the Epicurean*, when for a while he stepped out, with every appearance of determination, in society, but withdrew gratefully to his Oxford seclusion. For Pater, 'sensibility' — the power of profoundly experiencing what is significant in life and art — does for the artist the work done by a coarser, apriorist morality in society at large. Art, indeed, is life at its most intense and significant, "the products of the imagination must themselves be held to present the most perfect forms of life", we are told in *Marius*; art is what is significant in life, and so sensibility or insight, corruptible as it is, is the organ of moral knowledge, and art, for all its refusal to worship the *idola* of vulgar morality, is the only true morality; indeed it is nothing less than life itself. The artist or the 'aesthete', so elevated above all others, 'refines' the instruments of 'intuition' till his 'whole nature' becomes 'one complex medium of reception; what he receives is the vision — the 'beatific vision', if we cared to make it such — of our actual experience in the world." To achieve this, which is "not the conveyance of an abstract body of truths or principles" but "the conveyance of an art", demands an intense individuality, a cultivation of difference, and indeed conflict with the world at large. "It was intelligible that this 'aesthetic' philosophy might find itself. . . weighing the claims of that eager, concentrated, impassioned realization of experience against those of received morality", possibly it might even be (and here Pater could have been less carefully conditional), "as Pascal says of the kindly and temperate wisdom of Montaigne, 'pernicious for those who have any natural tendency to impiety or vice' ".

Pater returns with some evidence of anxiety to this possibly dangerous nonconformity; Marius comes to see the cost of this specialization to its devotees: "if now and then, they apprehended the world in its fullness, and had a vision, almost 'beatific', of ideal personalities in life and art, yet these moments were a very costly matter: they paid a great price for them, in the sacrifice of a thousand possible sympathies, from which they detached themselves, in intellectual pride. . ." If we want to know more about this 'vision', we have to return to the description of art as intensified life — "spirit and matter alike under their purest and most perfect conditions". At some time in the past (Pater blames the schoolmen, though there is no good reason for saddling them with the responsibility) it became habitual to establish a false opposition between spirit and matter. In the truly apprehended experience they are not dissociated; in the 'vision' they are inseparably fused. The form, in fact, of the work of art is not dissociable from its matter. "The mind", says Pater in the essay on Winckelmann, "begins and ends with the first image, yet loses no part of the spiritual motive. That motive is not loosely or lightly attached to the sensuous form, but saturates and is identical with it." This, of course, is what gives music its status as the art to which all the others aspire; it resists the separation of matter and form. Pater's thought about his 'vision' — it is the Image which is the subject of this essay — is well summed up by Mr. Graham Hough in the chapter on Pater in his book *The Last Romantics:* "His ideal is the kind of art where thought and its sensible embodiment are completely fused." Discourse is purged; the Image is the wisdom of Moneta, and it is a wisdom available only at great cost to the artist. Pater has his emblems of this costly wisdom, as Keats had the face of Moneta; and to him we shall return when such emblems come to be considered in themselves.

Between Wordsworth's account of 'sensibility' and Pater's, it will be observed that a far-reaching change has occurred. For Pater the 'sensibility' is the organ not merely of fine feeling but of moral discrimination and perception. The metaphysics of Coleridge crosses and diverts the simplicity of what Wordsworth, preceded by the empirical psychologists of the previous century, and succeeded by J. S. Mill, had believed: namely, that the higher degree of sensory organisation which distinguished poets from other men was fundamentally only a way of seeing and feeling *more*, not of seeing and feeling *differently*, and that it was a morally dangerous gift because it made it hard for the artist to be dully cautious about the satisfaction of his sensual appetites. Mill in particular seems to have correlated the necessarily high degree of 'sensibility' in artists with a certain intellectual immaturity, in Shelley for instance. And this, of course, is completely different from Pater's position; he maintains, in effect, that the estranged morality of artists is the only genuine kind. Now it is well known that Pater's account of the tension between the wisdom of the Image and a more utilitarian knowledge, between the artist's and the received morality, were gospel to the 'tragic generation'; and for all their perversity, for all their inferiority to these great predecessors, that generation transmitted the doctrine to the twentieth century and fed the imagination of its major poet.

No one has written better than Yeats about that generation of poets who "had to face their ends when young" — about Wilde, who so admired "The Crucifixion of the Outcast", about Dowson, and Johnson, who was to become crucial to Yeats's own developing idea of isolation. When the outcast counts on being crucified, indeed savours the prospect; when, bitter and gay, he abstains from morality for fear, as Yeats put it in a late letter, of losing the indispensable "heroic ecstasy", then we know we are dealing with a tradition which has become fully, not to say histrionically, self-conscious. A movement is strong when a man like Henley throws himself into an antithetical, activist movement, to oppose it. ("To converse with him," said Wilde after Henley had thrown him out of a café, "is a physical no less than an intellectual recreation.")

If we suspect the testimony of those who were all too deeply involved, we may turn to the detached, ironical, adverbial James; who, asked by the *Yellow Book* for a story, immediately began his own investigation into the relation between the quality of the work and the estrangement of its maker. As Mr. Blackmur has said, James saw the artist as an interesting theme for fiction only in his guise as a failure. If *life* is important, why be an artist? "It's so poor — so poor! . . .I mean as compared with being a person of action — as living your works." The young artist in *The Lesson of the Master*, who is in a sense James's

Callicles, may protest against this plight; but the Empedoclean Master has his answer ready:

"What a false position, what a condemnation of the artist, that he's a mere disenfranchised monk and can produce his effect only by giving up personal happiness! What an arraignment of art!" Paul went on with trembling voice.
"Ah, you don't imagine by chance that I'm defending art? 'Arraignment' — I should think so! Happy the societies in which it hasn't made its appearance, for from the moment it comes they have a consuming ache, they have an incurable corruption in their breast. Most assuredly the artist is in a false position! But I thought we were taking him for granted. . ."

The life these artists want, and which the older of them achieves at the cost of corrupting his art, is appallingly seductive; it is represented by the girl the young man desires and the older man marries, and by "the life she embodied, the young purity and richness of which appeared to imply that real success was to resemble *that*, to bloom, to present the perfection of a fine type, not to have hammered out headachy fancies with a bent back at an ink-stained table". Allowing for the difference of accent, this might be Yeats speaking. A man may choose (if indeed there is a choice) perfection of the life or of the work; and, as Yeats believed, the latter choice meant sacrifice, self-sacrifice. Marchbanks in *Candida* is absurd and embarrassing; but like him, the poet of the 'nineties was doomed, if not for the sake of the future for which Marchbanks was to legislate, then simply to guarantee his lonely access to the Image.

Lionel Johnson, the friend of Yeats, was in some ways the most distinguished of these poets. Yeats's many accounts of him dwell upon those elements in Johnson's life which he came increasingly to regard as typical. It is of Johnson he thinks first when he considers the dissipation and despair that are the inevitable lot of the modern artist, who must live in a world where what Yeats called Unity of Being is impossible — a world of division, where body and mind work separately, not moving as one, where the artist's motive and subject is his struggle with himself. When Yeats was young he used to write in autograph albums the famous words of Axel (later he substituted "For wisdom is a butterfly and not a gloomy bird of prey"). In 1899 he admiringly credited Johnson with Axel's attitude. "He has renounced the world and built up a twilight world instead. . . He might have cried out with Axel, 'As for living, our servants will do that for us' ". It was *Marius*, said Yeats, that had taught Johnson's generation "to walk upon a rope"; for as life demanded extravagant participation, art required isolation. These men, whom he later groups in his lunar system as "belonging by nature to the nights near the full", nade, says Yeats, what Arnold called "that morbid effort", and "suffered in their lives because of it". Formerly there had been ways of escape — Yeats's image for one of them is the Christian Thebaid — but these existed no more. Johnson might brood upon sanctity, but the Christian confessor cannot order a man not to be an artist, when "the whole life is art and poetry". "Full of the Image, he could never have that empty heart which calls the Hound of Heaven." And Johnson took pleasure in his doom, and in the torment he experienced because "some half-conscious part of him desired the world he had renounced"; he and Dowson "had the gravity of men who had found life out and were awakening from the dream". Johnson 'fell' constantly; not only in the moral sense, but downstairs, off stools, brooding upon sanctity as he did so; but when Yeats calls him "much-falling" he almost certainly has in mind that poem so much admired by Dowson, called 'Mystic and Cavalier', which is quoted in the *Autobiographies:*

> Go from me: I am one of those who fall. . .
>
> And in the battle, when the horsemen sweep
> Against a thousand deaths and fall on sleep:
> Who ever sought that sudden calm if I
> Sought not? Yet, could not die.

That such a poem exhausts action, that art exhausts life, was a notion that haunted Yeats: "Exhausted by the cry that it can never end, my love ends," he says magnificently in *A Vision*; and the song in *Resurrection* says the same thing. Johnson drained his life away into art, looking forward, with a kind of tragic irony, to ten years on when he would be ruined, begging from his friends; but he fell once too often before the time was up. What of the artist who continues to exist, preying gloomily upon the substance of his own life? Age merely confirms his abstraction, his exclusion from ordinary vitality, by turning him into a scarecrow. Age is as hateful as the headache and the cough, the inky laborious craft — Adam's curse — whether the artist be young or old. "My first denunciation of old age," said Yeats, "I made before I was twenty." Indeed the antithesis of living man and creator was one of the root assumptions of his life and work; he drew the artist as a tragic hero, proving life by the act of withdrawing from it. He was of the great conspiracy of contemplative men, and had made his choice of "perfection of the work"; but he retained and developed a harrowing sense of the goodness of life and action, and a conviction that "real success was to resemble *that*".

"Art is solitary man," wrote J. B. Yeats to his son, in the midst of their rich wartime correspondence. At that time, the poet was obviously unhappy about his abstinence from the exceptionally violent contemporary life of action; he had a taste for such violence, satisfied later when affable irregulars frequented Thoor Ballylee, and gunfights went on round the offices of Dublin, but in the English war he could not even play a poet's part. At such a time his father's emphasis on the proper detachment of the artist must have been agreeable. "All art is *reaction from life*," said J. B. Yeats, "but never, when it is vital and great, *an escape*. . . In Michelangelo's time it was not possible to escape for life was there every *minute* as real as the toothache and as terrible and impressive as the judgment day." This is a very Yeatsian formula. Yet, whatever the quality of life he has to deal with, "the poet is the antithesis of the man of action". He does not "meddle in ethics"; he is a magician, "his dreams shall have a potency to defeat the actual at every point" — this is the poet *versus* the universe of death, the world of reason.

Art exists that man cutting himself away from nature may build in his free consciousness buildings vaster and more sumptuous than these [the 'habitations of ease and comfort'] built by science; furnished too with all manner of winding passages and closets and boudoirs and encircled with gardens well shaded and with everything he can desire — and we build all out of our spiritual pain — for if the bricks be not cemented and mortised by actual suffering, they will not hold together. Those others live on another plane, where if there is less joy there is much less pain. . . The artist. . . out of his pain and humiliations constructs for himself habitations, and if she [Nature] sweeps them away with a blow of her hand he only builds them afresh, and as his joy is chiefly in the act of building he does not mind how often he has to do it.

Here, apart from the dubious connotations of the architectural analogy, we have something close to the essence of the younger Yeats's résumé of the tradition. What, after all, is the *Vision*, but a blueprint of a palace of art, a place in the mind where men may suffer, some less and some more, where the artist explains his joy in making at the cost of isolation and suffering? The joy of building is the same thing as Yeats's brief victory, the creation of an antithesis for fate. The father admitted his intellectual debt to his son; but nobody could have restated the Romantic case so suitably to the son's purposes.

The free, self-delighting intellect which knows that pain is the cost of its joy; the licence to look inward and paint, as Blake and Palmer painted, a symbolic world; to make a magical explanation of a divine order — all this represents the victory of Coleridge, of Blake and the French; it is the heritage, delightful and tragic, to which Yeats was born. Much in his own life made him kick against the pricks; his love of aristocratic skills, of the achievements of others in the sphere of action, of his own successes in the active life. Out of this oscillation between the two states of life came the desire, natural to a magician, to tame by explaining, to answer the question, why are men different, and why are men divided? But long before Yeats ventured on his schematic explanations he had been concerned in a more general way with the justification of the ways of the artist and the defence of poetry.

The development of Yeats's cluster of ideas about the status of the artist in life is complex, and some aspects of it I here almost ignore. But I must say something about it, because it culminates in the elegy on Robert Gregory which is the subject of the next chapter, and because it is an indispensable preliminary to any discussion of Yeats's conception of the work of art itself. So certain was he that art was not 'escape' that he thought of the situation the other way round: art was what you tried to escape from. The failure of Wilde to understand this was, for Yeats, something to be explained only by taking Wilde out of the ranks of the artists altogether. It was because he hated the conventional notion of 'escape' that Yeats was early troubled by that dreaminess, that conscientious lack of actuality, which prevailed when he made his début; he was trying to shake it off much earlier than is usually supposed, trying to get strong, living rhythms and a language "as subtle, as complex, as full of mysterious life, as the body of a flower or of a woman". He grew suspicious of a kind of covert sensuality in this Romantic dream. We may be grateful that he did; the extension of his range, the cult of a language of organic rhythms and of great rhetorical variety, are what made him a great poet. But for all that, he never ceased to subscribe to the old doctrine that art is a kind of dream, and that to dream it well is the most difficult and exhausting of all callings. Great art unifies sense and spirit, like the body of a beautiful woman, or like a portrait by Titian, or like Donne's Elizabeth Drury; but the age was unpropitious, the available method faulty and in need of revision. The tradition is not to be sacrificed; all that is potent and valid in it is to be preserved, though in a new form.

In *A Vision*, Yeats wrote of "an early conviction of mine that the creative power of the lyric poet depends upon his accepting some of a few traditional attitudes, lover, sage, hero, scorner of life"; and as early as *The Celtic Twilight* he describes a Symbolist vision, of apes eating jewels in hell, which contains the elements of what later became a powerful and immediate impulse. "I knew that I saw the Celtic Hell, and my own Hell, the Hell of the artist, and that all who sought after beautiful and wonderful things with too avid a thirst, lost peace and form, and became shapeless and common." Here, in embryo, is the story of the cost to the artist of what Yeats, in an early essay entitled 'Poetry and the Tradition', calls his unique "continual and self-delighting happiness"; it turns the dedicated, however pretty their plumage, into old scarecrows, and excludes them from life. Hanrahan, of whom the poet was to speak again in the isolation of the Tower, — "leave Hanrahan, For I need all his mighty memories" — is tricked into leaving the dance of life, just as he was coming to where comfort was. Later he composed a great curse on old age; he had been touched by the Sidhe — a Yeatsian figure for the dedication, voluntary or no, of the artist — and had to pay the cost. The poet is not like the others. Joy makes him free for his task of stitching and unstitching, of labour at the higher reality of the imagination. But this labour is what ruins life, makes the body shapeless and common. Solitude grows with what Yeats calls the growing absorption of the dream; the long series of indecisive victories, "intellectual recreations of all that exterior fate snatches away", increase it further and torment the poet. His fate is a ruined life, intermittently illuminated by the Image. Poets and artists, says Yeats in *Per Amica Silentia Lunae*, "must go from desire to weariness and so to desire again, and live for the moment when vision comes like terrible lightning, in the humility of the brutes". Tormented by the necessary failure of his life, appalled in conscience or in vanity, he can say, "I suffered continual remorse, and only became content when my abstractions had composed themselves into picture and dramatisation". This content is impermanent; the poet is thus perpetually divided against himself. Hence the distinction Yeats makes "between the perfection that is from a man's combat with himself and that which is from a combat with circumstance". Behind it lies the hopeless anger of an artist in love with action, with life. This occupied Yeats incessantly, and it is hardly too much to say that it informs most of his later poetry as well as his universal history, which is, virtually, an attempt to make all history an explanation of why the modern artist is isolated.

A young poet, encountering for the first time the *fertilisante douleur* and the massive indifference of the public, might be aware of the pressure of problems similar to his own in the poetry of Yeats without grasping the fullness of Yeats's statement, the institutional — one might almost say apostolic — quality of this poet, which places the enthusiastic anti-Romanticism of a Hulme as a heresy, the sad heresy of the slightly misinformed, who seek a primitive purity with eyes blinded by tradition. The modern truth about the poet's difference, about that stern injunction, "No road through to action", about the problem of communication — how and to whom? — is in Yeats, in a rich and perfected context. He is the poet in whose work Romantic isolation achieves its full quality as a theme for poetry, being no longer a pose, a complaint, or a programme; and his treatment of it is very closely related to his belief in what Pater called 'vision' and the French called Symbol. He does not deny the pain that is terminated momentarily by the daily victory, permanently by death; indeed the fascination of this last, fierce solution was as apparent to him as to Moritz and some of the French writers. He simply understands it more fully than anybody else, in its relation to the Image. That is why there is so much about Yeats in what follows. The poem that gives us the best start is his elegy, 'In Memory of Major Robert Gregory', and to that work I devote the next chapter.

II

'IN MEMORY OF
MAJOR ROBERT GREGORY'

Have you noticed that when we talk of a man of
genius we try to explain his failure?
All contemplative men are in a conspiracy to
overrate their state of life, and . . .all great writers
are of them excepting the great poets.

J. B. YEATS

'IN Memory of Major Robert Gregory' is Yeats's first full
statement of what he took to be a complex and tragic
situation: the position of artists and contemplatives in a
world built for action, and their chances of escape, which are
in effect two, the making of Images, and death. It is a poem
worthy of much painful reading, perhaps the first in which we
hear the full range of the poet's voice; and with this heroic
assurance of harmony goes an authentic mastery of design.
After it, for twenty years, Yeats's poems, whenever he is using
his whole range, are identifiable as the work of the master of
the Gregory elegy.

A poem which has these indications of centrality deserves to
be supplied with appropriate contexts, and to be asked the
proper questions. Such questions, of course, need never end,
and there must be arbitrary limits set to any fit of interroga-
tion. At any rate, I can promise the reader that this is not an
exercise in Yeatsian schematics. It is, I think, profitable to
begin with a straightforward account of how the elegy came
to be written.

Yeats celebrates many times his rich friendship with Lady

Gregory. "Infernally haughty" his father called her; but, he adds, "on the whole I am glad that Lady G. 'got' Willie". Certainly she gave Yeats sustenance for more than his proliferating aristocratic fantasies; she could share with little effort his "dream of the noble and the beggarman". Their friendship was ceremonious and intimate; she gave him all he needed of the aristocratic intellect, her inheritance of assured patrician nonchalance; and he never wavered from the integrity she required of nobleman, peasant and poet. In 1924, when Yeats got his Nobel prize, she wrote, with more than usual warmth, in her diary, "I am proud and glad of this triumph for I believed in him always and was glad 'he never made a poorer song that he might have a heavier purse'. In these 26 years our friendship has never been broken". As collaborator and friend she must have been too close for even Yeats to mythologize her, to make her part of any magical scheme save that of the all too obviously dying order, of that calm and arrogant aristocracy which was rich without selling itself for the money. Her brothers he did make a legend of; they were the gentlemen of a better age for poets:

> We too had good attendance once,
> Hearers and hearteners of the work;
> Aye, horsemen for companions,
> Before the merchant and the clerk
> Breathed on the world with timid breath,

and for her only son Robert he had a warm affection; the young man was brave and gifted, a scholar, a horseman and a painter. As a scenic designer he had worked with Yeats at the Abbey, and he had been consulted about the conversion of Thoor Ballylee, the ruined Norman tower near the Gregory estate, which Yeats had bought in 1917. Gregory painted the Tower (the painting is reproduced in Hone's biography of Yeats).

Before either the Tower or its adjacent cottage were ready for habitation Gregory, who had joined the Royal Flying Corps, was killed on the Italian front on 23rd January, 1918. In June of that year, when preparations for moving into the Tower were almost complete, Yeats wrote 'In Memory of Major Robert Gregory', the first poem of many to use the Tower as a poetical property. We may here remind ourselves

31

that the Tower as a symbol has wide and fluctuating contexts in Yeats, but its root signification is the isolation of the artist.

Half a year had passed between the death of Gregory and the writing of this poem, but during that time it appears that Yeats dwelt much upon the event. On 8th February, having heard the news from Lady Gregory, he wrote to John Quinn:

> News will have reached you before this of Robert Gregory's death in action. I feel it very much for his own sake, still more for his mother's. I think he had genius. Certainly no contemporary landscape moved me as much as two or three of his, except perhaps a certain landscape by Innes, from whom he had learnt a good deal. His paintings had majesty and austerity, and at the same time sweetness. He was the most accomplished man I have ever known; he could do more things than any other. He had proved himself a most daring airman, having been particularly successful in single combat with German planes. . .

Here is the germ of what was to come later. Yeats thinks of Gregory first as an artist; then of his uniquely varied powers, which suggest what was for Yeats a paradox, the simultaneous possession of mastery in the spheres of both action and contemplation. We shall see that, as he sorted out his interests in the dead man, Yeats came to regard this paradox as having most to do with his own poetry.

At about the same time as this letter to Quinn, Yeats contributed an obituary notice of Gregory to *The Observer*. This notice is worth reprinting in full because it is more highly organized and suggestive than the letter to Quinn.

> I have known no man accomplished in so many ways as Major Robert Gregory, who was killed in action a couple of weeks ago and buried by his fellow-airmen in the beautiful cemetery at Padua. His very accomplishment hid from many his genius. He had so many sides: painter, classical scholar, scholar in painting and in modern literature, boxer, horseman, airman — he had the M.C. and the Légion d'Honneur — that some among his friends were not sure what his work would be. To me he will always remain a great painter in the immaturity of his youth, he himself the personification of handsome youth. I first came to understand his genius

when, still almost a boy, he designed for Lady Gregory's *Kinkora* and her *Image* and for my *Shadowy Waters* and for Synge's *Deirdre of the Sorrows* decorations which, obtaining their effect from the fewest possible lines and colours, had always the grave distinction of his own imagination. When he began to paint, accustomed to an older school of painting I was long perplexed by what seemed to me neglect of detail. But in a few years I came to care for his paintings of the Clare coast, with its cloudy shadows upon blue-grey stony hills, and for one painting of a not very different scenery by his friend, Innes, more than for any contemporary landscape painting. A man of letters may perhaps find in work such as this, or in old Chinese painting, in the woodcuts and etchings of Calvert and Palmer, in Blake's woodcuts to Thornton's *Virgil*, in the landscape background of Mr. Ricketts' *Wise and Foolish Virgins*, something that he does not find in the great modern masters, and that he cares for deeply. Is it merely that these men share certain moods with great lyric poetry, with, let us say, *The Leech Gatherer* of Wordsworth; or that their moods, unlike those of men with more objective curiosity, are a part of the traditional expression of the soul? One always understands by something in his selection of line and colour that he had read his Homer and his Virgil and his Dante; that they, while giving something of themselves, had freed him from easy tragedy and trivial comedy.

Though he often seemed led away from his work by some other gift, his attitude to life and art never lost intensity — he was never the amateur. I have noticed that men whose lives are to be an ever-growing absorption in subjective beauty — and I am not merely remembering Calvert's philosophy of myth and his musical theory, or Verlaine's sensuality, or Shelley's politics — seek through some lesser gift, or through mere excitement, to strengthen that self which unites them with ordinary men. It is as though they hesitated before they plunged into the abyss. Major Gregory told Mr. Bernard Shaw, who visited him in France, that the months since he joined the army had been the happiest of his life. I think they brought him peace of mind, an escape from that shrinking, which I sometimes saw upon his face, before the growing absorption of his dream, as from his

constant struggle to resist those other gifts that brought him
ease and friendship. Leading his squadron in France or in
Italy, mind and hand were at one, will and desire.

The almost casual magniloquence of these lines conceals a
series of assumptions which were of extraordinary importance
to Yeats, and to his understanding of the tradition in which he
worked; and they further suggest the way in which he was
already systematizing Gregory, making his memory the node
of much complicated speculation. The extreme variety of
Gregory's accomplishment is antithetical to the singleness of
the fate he struggles to escape; Yeats, in fact, settles rather
arbitrarily upon Gregory's power as a painter, calls it the
prime calling of the young man, and describes all the rest as
distraction, more or less voluntarily pursued in a world of
movement and friendship, but bound, unless the process be
interrupted by the most decisive of all acts, to absorb the artist
completely. He admires the rich diversity of aristocratic talent,
of course; in fact it occupied his mind from the first, but as the
myth of Gregory grew, the poet's insistence upon this aspect
declined. The greater part of the *Observer* obituary is concerned with the placing of Gregory as a painter in a certain tradition; and this is the tradition of Blake, as expounded by Yeats
years before in the essay called 'Symbolism in Painting'. Miss
Marion Witt has written well about Yeats's concern, at the
time of Gregory's death, with Palmer and Calvert. When the
news reached him Yeats was in Oxford, his table in the Bodlei-
an strewn with their works. He was reviving his interest in
Calvert's theory of myth, and in the pronouncements of these
artists concerning the symbolic quality of landscape, and the
creative meditation which redeems the universe of death;
relating them not only to Blake, but to the Wordsworth of the
archetypal Romantic poem of meditation, 'Resolution and
Independance'. And this is the tradition — note his insistence
upon its literary connexions — in which Yeats understood
himself to be working. His emphasis on Blake's importance in
it is a natural consequence of his part in the Blake revival.
Gregory was to have been a maker of symbols, of images perceptible to the Blakean eye. And it follows that he was to have
been *different*, isolated, cut off from life and action. Gregory,
we are told, was no amateur, but a dedicated or doomed (it is

the same thing in the end) professional. He sought to escape by
feats of the body, by an elegant scholarship; but in the end only death — the means of which were therefore delightful to
him — could release him, liberate him from the 'growing absorption of his dream'. Others before him had made their
momentary escapes: Calvert into his system, Verlaine (a minor
hero of Yeats's, as we shall see) into the honeypot of Paris. But
Gregory alone of them found a definitive joy in abandoning
the pain and delight of the dream for self-destructive action.

The whole obituary, save for the opening tribute to easy
aristocratic skills, concerns Gregory as artist, growing into
isolation, escaping from it with a strange and violent delight.
Whatever the truth may have been about Gregory as an artist,
there is certainly no doubt about this delight; as Yeats in
middle age prepared his Tower, where his lamp would burn
for the truth that comes from the tomb, the young artist forgot
the powers that were possessing him and found an active joy.
"The way to be happy," wrote J. B. Yeats, "is to forget yourself. That is why Robert Gregory was happy."

Because we know how early Yeats began to shape the poetic
significance of his friend, we may be surprised that his first
attempts to celebrate the dead man's memory appear largely
to ignore this significance. Already in February, 1918, he was
thinking about a poem on Gregory's death. "I am trying to
write something in verse about Robert," he said in a letter to
Lady Gregory on 22nd. February, "but do not know what will
come. I am trying a poem in manner like one that Spenser
wrote for Sir Philip Sidney." At this stage Yeats sees his poem
as concerned mainly with Gregory's courtesy, thinking of him
as a soldier-scholar born out of his time, a man who might have
praised Pugliano and graced the intellectual sweetness of the
talk at Urbino. And certainly, when he considered the history
of European culture, cankered by false education, hopeless in
disunity, — this was how he thought about men like Gregory.
There was also, perhaps, a pleasing propriety in his playing
Spenser to Gregory's Sidney; and so the pastoral poem called
'Shepherd and Goatherd' was his first attempt at an elegy for
his friend. It was finished on March 19th, when Yeats wrote
thus to Lady Gregory: "I have today finished my poem about
Robert, a pastoral, modelled on what Virgil wrote for some
friend of his, and what Spenser wrote on Sidney. My wife

thinks it good. A goatherd and a shepherd are talking in some vague place, perhaps the Burren hills, in some remote period of the world. It is a new form for me, and I think for modern poetry."

Yeats's critical interest in earlier poetry was sensitive and profound, but eccentric. He had not that conventional education which, for all its merits as a preparation for poetry, perhaps tends to impose a critic's rather than a poet's view of the past. He was less interested in the subtle laws of *genre* than in specific effects and achievements, and he did not read Spenser's elegy as Milton and Shelley must have done. Where they saw a richly suggestive conventional form, so that every line of a new pastoral elegy might arouse privileged echoes of Theocritus, Bion and Virgil, Yeats saw rather a device for ensuring an aristocratic distance between the poet and his subject, a possibility of achieving an interesting stoic coldness, as of carved flames. The best he could hope to achieve in the pastoral elegy would be this monumental apathy; or perhaps he also felt that he could bring together aristocrat and shepherd, Irish scholar-hero and Irish peasant-poet, by means of the pastoral artifice. But where Spenser could not escape frigidity, and Milton (another poet who wished all to run in an unfashionable gyre) could not escape the charge of it, Yeats could not succeed. Most agree that 'Shepherd and Goatherd' is a bad poem. We study at a distance what cannot engage us. The pastoral fiction sorts ill with fragments of the mythology or 'system' upon which Yeats was at the time working. Where there is leisure for *mystizismus*, there is little, we feel, for grief. Later in his life Yeats wrote that his poetry was full of his 'private philosophy', adding that "there must be no sign of it; all must be like an old fairy tale". But in this poem the system is coldly obvious; we are asked to take both the pastoral and the passages concerning the dead man's retreat from sense — "knowledge he shall unwind/Through victories of the mind" — at more than their face value; it looks poor and it is poor.

But the basic reason for the failure is probably that Yeats's important feelings about Gregory *as an artist* were as yet unformed. The rich possibilities of the *Observer* obituary remained unrealised. Yeats must quickly have seen this, for he was a great maker of elegies, and his subjects — dead, or dead to him, through "wine or women, or some curse" — were never ripe until they had entered the flesh and blood of his thought. They are all changed; there is no lament that simply presents the loss of a woman, or a friend, or a political martyr, without making them part of a mood or a myth. But here Yeats has not made the loss of Gregory a part of the world of his mind's making, and the poem lies bizarre among the insignificant realities of the commonplace vision; it lacks 'the grave distinction of his own imagination'. In short, Yeats was not yet wholly engaged by the Gregory theme.

The short poem 'An Irish Airman Foresees his Death' was probably written before the great elegy. It treats of Gregory's exultant happiness in his war career, a delight momentous for Yeats's developed thinking about his friend, and which is not mentioned at all in the pastoral elegy.

> Nor law nor duty bade me fight,
> Nor public men, nor cheering crowds;
> A lonely impulse of delight
> Drove to this tumult in the clouds;
> I balanced all, brought all to mind,
> The years to come seemed waste of breath,
> A waste of breath the years behind
> In balance with this life, this death.

The impulse is from within; it is an impulse to resolve the tension between the growing absorption of the dream and the desire for society and the pleasures of action. For a moment an equilibrium is achieved; the tensions resolved, there is life, life of extraordinary fulness; but at the cost, the world being what it is, of immediate extinction. This unifying and destructive delight, the singular achievement by a gifted artist of unity at the expense of life itself, is a leading motive in the great elegy which Yeats wrote in the summer, as he prepared to take possession of the Tower. "I do nothing but write verse," he wrote to his father on 14th June, "and have just finished a long poem in memory of Major Robert Gregory, which is among my best works."

Of 'In Memory of Major Robert Gregory' itself, it would be tedious to offer another *explication*; it has been well studied by Miss Witt and by Mr. Peter Ure in his *Towards a Mythology* (1946). With the manifold symbolism of the Tower developing in his mind — it was not only the sign of the contemplative, of a dying order, of the modern world 'half-dead at the top', but it stood in Gregory country, and the young man was intimately associated with it — Yeats saw Gregory clear for the first time; he saw him as primarily the artist who had escaped into action, a delighted escape from a typical cruel dilemma imposed by the nature of the artist and exacerbated by modern decadence; and this escape was made by a way which other divided men had not found, or had not risked. These other men were important to Yeats. Pollexfen, once active, "had no enterprise but in contemplation", when age defeated his physical force. Johnson and Synge were "always at his side": Synge, obsessed like Gregory with the inward growing of dream and Image, so that Yeats enjoined him to make his escape; Johnson the formal antithesis of Gregory in his solution.

I speak as though Gregory were treated in this poem as an artist-contemplative and as nothing else; and this is almost true. The richness and variety of his powers are there, of course; he is "our Sidney and our perfect man", "soldier, scholar, horseman"; death, in a beautiful conceit, does him not an injury but an ill-bred discourtesy; and Yeats, still casting about among the personal elegies of the Renaissance, had chosen Cowley's elegy for a scholar who was not, like Sidney, a man of action, as his model. The much-admired stanza of 'In Memory of Major Robert Gregory', and of such later poems as 'A Prayer for my Daughter' and the second poem in the 'Tower' sequence, is not an invention of Yeats, but a borrowing from Cowley. Yeats did not forget the connexion between Gregory and the perfect man of the Renaissance, whose diverse accomplishments were also brought to unity under the burning glass of chivalrous war. Nor had he forgotten that the Renaissance had its elegies, not all of them pastoral; and his eye fell upon, or his memory recalled, Cowley's famous 'Ode on the Death of Mr. William Harvey'.

> It was a dismal and a fearful Night,
> Scarce could the morn drive on th' unwilling Light,
> When *Sleep, Deaths,* Image, left my troubled breast
>   By something *liker Death* possest.
> My Eyes with Tears did uncommanded flow,
>   And on my Soul hung the dull weight
>   Of some *Intolerable Fate*.
> What Bell was that? Ah me! Too much I know . . . .

Say, for you saw us, ye Immortal *Lights,*
How oft unweary'd have we spent the Nights?
Till the *Ledæan Stars* so fam'd for love
    Wonder'd at us from above.
We spent them not in Toys, in Lusts, or Wine;
    But search of deep *Philosophy,*
    Wit, Eloquence, and *Poetry;*
Arts which I lov'd, for they, my *Friend,* were *Thine* ....

So strong a *Wit* did *Nature* to him frame,
As all things but his *Judgment* overcame;
His *Judgment* like the Heav'nly *Moon* did show,
    Temp'ring that Mighty *Sea* below.
O had he liv'd in *Learning's World,* what Bound
    Would have been able to controul
    His over-pow'ring Soul?
We've lost in him *Arts* that not yet are found ....

Cowley's characteristically uneven, over-long and over-witty poem lacks the design of Yeats's, and what structure it has is partly prefabricated, deriving from the conventional Renaissance funeral elegy, which is both schematic and witty. But, as far as I know, Cowley invented the stanza, and having seen Yeats use it, we may be prepared to grant that it has great virtue. It has balance and variety, and in the long concluding line Cowley began an experiment in the elegiac possibilities of slow, heavily retarded monosyllabic movement, which Yeats was happy to continue. Cowley often succeeds:

> Dark as the grave wherein my friend is laid
> Mute as the grave wherein my friend does lie
> And this my grief without thy help shall write
> Nor could his ink flow faster than his wit;

but Yeats never fails:

> All, all are in my thoughts tonight being dead
> For all that come into my mind are dead
> As though he had but that one trade alone
> What made us dream that he could comb grey hair;

and above all the last line of the poem, the clustered consonants grievously impeding utterance:

>   but the thought
> Of that late death took all my heart for speech.

Yeats here practises a poet's, not a critic's imitation. William Harvey was not a Sidney, but he was, according to Cowley, a many-sided genius who died young, and the poem which commemorates him struck certain chords that interested Yeats; he therefore imitated it. In so doing, he achieves as it were unconsciously the formal link with the Renaissance hero that he had unsuccessfully tried for in the pastoral. He took from Cowley, as a poet of the Renaissance man, precisely what the unborn poem required, the stanza, the repetitive devices, some perhaps of the funeral wit; these would help him to achieve that balance of remoteness and distraught familiarity which the pastoral had not given him, and which Cowley achieved by his combination of slow rhythms and colloquial language. Yeats may also have liked the motto of Cowley's poem, drawn from Martial: *Immodicis brevis est aetas, et rara senectus*. The Roman poet is using the word *immodicus* with a pathetic irony: normally it means 'one given to excess', but Martial is lamenting the death of a beautiful and accomplished slave-boy. For Cowley's purposes one could translate the line, "For men of genius life is short, and old age rare," but for Yeats's one would have to recover the original idea of excess: "To those who are too accomplished. . ." or even "too variously accomplished". In any case, Cowley's elegy helped to indicate the form which Yeats's material sought, and it brought to a happy issue that preoccupation with Sidney and the Renaissance elegy which was forced on the poet, and which for a time impeded his full exploration of the significance of Gregory's death as the artist's escape.

For this is the main theme of the elegy. Apart from the stanza about Gregory's foolhardy horsemanship, the poem treats its subject virtually as a painter only; and Miss Witt is able to inform us that this stanza was added later to satisfy Mrs. Gregory's objection that not enough was said in the poem about her husband's physical courage. The omission of that stanza leaves us with a clearer development from the landscape of Thoor Ballylee to the greatness of the painter of cold Clare rock, stern colour and delicate line. The poem is probably improved by the change. The accomplishments of Gregory which are actually described are all in the plastic arts. It is as an artist — though with the old aristocratic *sprezzatura* — escaping from the penalties of imagination, that the dead man is presented to us. This is a symbolic figure, violently abstracted from life, existing in some pattern of the poet's mind as independently of the particularities of ordinary perception as the Leech Gatherer, standing in some special relationship to the other artists of the poem that only the poem itself can fully explain.

Yeats returned once more to the theme of Gregory's death, in an angry little poem written, but not published, in 1921. In it he addresses his friend as one who had died for the country whose soldiers, only three years later, were ravaging his estate and ill-treating his peasantry. Gregory is once again the typical generous aristocrat, though now among the "cheated dead". The moment of the Elegy, when for Yeats he was an artist memorable because of his escape from the dream of estrangement, was past. The process by which Yeats narrowed down the significance of his friend's death to this is explicable only in terms of the tradition I have been discussing. In the great poem itself the dead man's soldiership and horsemanship, qualities which might seem to associate him with the life of action, are vestigial; they serve only as hints, to show how, in the teeth of the fate that was visibly overtaking him, he was able to achieve, in the life of action, that Unity of Being which is the ideal of the personal life, and which the present age denies. Even so, it was only at the cost of immediate extinction that Gregory achieved it, triumphantly consuming his dream, ending the oscillation of the poet devoted to the Image by ending the process of exile and giving himself to death; de Guérin would have understood the poem at once. Lionel Johnson is a necessary part of the myth; he had the archetypal longing for action, and he demonstrates the despair of the artist who does not win his daily victory; he suffered, as Huysmans suffered, for the sins of society. Gregory avoids this fate (as he avoids grey hair, that old age which Hanrahan cursed) by his Empedoclean solution. But there is a difference; escaping from the abyss of art, Gregory finds delight, life in death, by achieving "the perfection of a fine type". He transcends all partial, divided men, and becomes himself a radiant symbol, measuring and illuminating the whole collapsing world, and the artists who struggle to work in it. He becomes Yeats's victory. And this was only possible when he had been placed, as a painter, in the tradition of Blake and Calvert and Palmer, a tradition which, as Miss Witt says, was interesting Yeats at the time of Gregory's death, but which he had assimilated long before, as the essay called 'Symbolism and Painting' demonstrates. Calvert "is as much a symbolist as Blake or Wagner... he evokes in his landscapes an infinite emotion, a perfected emotion, a part of the Divine Essence"; he works by Imagination, imitating *natura naturans*, not *natura naturata*; his concern is with the dream, with the Imagination's echo of the great I am. For Yeats, the tradition was founded by Blake, so that to the aesthetic of Blake he had added what he conceived to be necessary magical justifications. "No Man of Sense," said Blake, "can think that an Imitation of the Objects of Nature is The Art of Painting"; announced thus by "the chanticleer of the new dawn", the tradition of symbolic landscape painting is the one in which Yeats would have wished to find his typical artist, his seer of the Image, if that artist were a painter. Gregory is carefully placed in it. Given his story, the rest of the myth follows, is easily suggested. Johnson "comes the first to mind", because he was so perfectly and so agonisedly what Gregory magnificently contrived not to be. Gregory escaped from art, and his escape became an image, a new thing named, a new truth, for an artist who did not escape but stood his course in a darkening and increasingly hostile world.

III

THE IMAGE

Those pests and parasites of artistic work - ideas.
GEORGE MOORE

It is even possible that being is only possessed by
the dead, and that it is some knowledge of this
that makes us gaze with so much emotion upon
the face of the Sphinx or the Buddha.
YEATS

So Gregory becomes, to speak for the moment with less
precision than may legitimately be demanded, a symbol;
the poem about him is for Yeats one of those victories by
which the artist lives in tragic solitude. He reconciles the
opposites of action and contemplation; and this reconciliation
of opposites, very properly in a Romantic poet, is the purpose
of the Yeatsian symbol, which is the flowering of what I call
the Romantic Image. (As throughout this essay I here use
'Romantic' in a restricted sense, as applicable to the literature
of one epoch, beginning in the late years of the eighteenth
century and not yet finished, and as referring to the high valuation placed during this period upon the image-making powers
of the mind at the expense of its rational powers, and to the
substitution of organicist for mechanistic modes of thinking
about works of art.)

Thus far I have spoken of process rather than product, and
it is now time to consider the work of art which is the victory,
the product of the pain and the joy. We shall find in accounts
of it an intense superficial confusion, but fundamentally the

43

unanimity of the witnesses is impressive. The work of art itself is symbol, 'aesthetic monad'; utterly original and not in the old sense 'imitated'; 'concrete', yet fluid and suggestive; a means to truth, a truth unrelated to, and more exalted than, that of positivist science, or any observation depending upon the discursive reason; out of the flux of life, and therefore, under one aspect, dead; yet uniquely alive because of its participation in a higher order of existence, and because it is analogous not to a machine but to an organism; coextensive in matter and form; resistant to explication; largely independent of intention, and of any form of ethical utility; and itself emblematised in certain recurring images, of which, as the next chapter shows, the Dancer is the most perfect. These formulae involve certain apparent contradictions — the work of art is under one aspect dead, under another alive, marble yet treelike, fixed yet constantly moving. Such are the superficial contradictions. Yet some such conception of the Image as that given in crabbed outline in this paragraph animates much of the best writing between Coleridge and Blake at the outset and Pound and Eliot in our own time.

It will be useful, though doubtless unexpected, to begin here with a glance at Wilde's dialogue, *The Critic as Artist*, irritating as most people now find it, because by ruthlessly abstracting some of its arguments we may be able to indicate some of the disguised similarities between poetic periods usually considered antithetical. Wilde's dialogue is full of affectedly exultant isolation, glorying in its symbolism of tower and mask, in the central figure of the dreamer whom society will never forgive. This dreamer of course needs some mode of communication; and he achieves it by grace of Imagination; for him as for Yeats and the magicians, Imagination is "concentrated race-experience". This is intimately related to the whole submerged magical system of Romantic aesthetic, about which Yeats and some Frenchmen were bold enough to be explicit. The object of the artist is to produce pleasure, though pleasure is a somewhat inadequate term; better to say that he has nothing to do with anything useful. "All the arts are immoral except those baser forms of sensual or didactic art that seek to excite to action of evil or of good." The word "immoral" here represents a coarsening of the aesthetic in the interests of paradox; but the descent of the idea is obvious enough, and Wilde is concerned, in modern terms, to distinguish art from both propaganda and entertainment, and to hang on it the sign "No road through to action". His opinion is exactly that of Stephen Dedalus in *The Portrait*. Wilde further denies the part of imitation; "all artistic creation is absolutely subjective. The very landscape that Corot looked at was, as he said himself, but a mood of his own mind". It might be Yeats speaking; it might, with certain metaphysical qualifications, be Coleridge; or, entirely rephrased, Blake. The passages on colour and line, on "the deliberate rejection of Nature", are only more emphatic ways of saying what Yeats says in his attacks on Nature for Nature's sake, and in his appreciations of Calvert, Palmer and Sickert; and what is rejected is the nature of things "in disconnexion dead and spiritless" abhorred of Coleridge and Wordsworth, the world of Blake's vegetative eye. Like Blake and Yeats, Wilde expressed his detestation of an educational system which cultivated memory rather than imagination, and taught people to remember, not how to grow. Having speculated sufficiently upon the image and its status, Wilde's young men go out into the *luministe*, purple-shadowed dawn, to see the morning's roses in Covent Garden.

Their mannered musings contain little that would have surprised Coleridge; but their ways of putting things have a particular interest for us. For Gilbert (Wilde's rather tiresome mouthpiece) the images of poetry have more 'reality' than action can have; for action dies at the moment of energy. In distinguishing, however, between the image in the plastic arts and the image in literature, he touches upon an issue which was to have considerable importance, for example in the aesthetics of Vortex. The distinction is made in this way.

> The statue is concentrated to one moment of perfection. The image stained upon the canvas possesses no spiritual element of growth or change. If they know nothing of death, it is because they know little of life, for the secrets of life and death belong to those and those only, whom the sequence of time affects, and who possess not merely the present but the future, and can rise or fall from a past of glory or of shame. Movement, that problem of the visible arts, can be truly realized by Literature alone. It is Literature that shows us the body in its swiftness and the soul in its unrest.

A passage of this kind, full of confusing ambiguities in key words like 'life' and 'death', 'movement', 'growth', 'body' and 'soul', would convince no modern critic, but is nevertheless more satisfying in some ways than influential pronouncements which explicitly identify the visual with the literary image; and there is a 'feeling' in the passage for the problem which Vortex tried to solve, and from which Yeats made great poems — a problem made up of the nexus of ambiguous relationships, by no means always seen steadily as a merely semantic challenge, existing between different senses of the word 'image', associated words like 'symbol', and related concepts like 'movement' and 'concretion'. Some parts of this complex we shall, more or less historically, look into; meanwhile there are other matters of interest in Wilde's dialogue.

The species of 'image' with which he is concerned cannot, of course, stand in any simple relation to merely "intellectual intention". (Both Wilde and Yeats disliked or distrusted the symbolism of Ibsen.) "When the work is finished it has, as it were, an independent life of its own [notice the habitual Romantic organicist analogy, which I discuss in Chapter V], and may deliver a message far other than that which was put into its lips to say." This is a perfectly logical anti-intentionalist position, and it is a fundamental one in all Romantic criticism, including what is known as the New Criticism of recent years. A corollary of this attitude to intellect (we are dealing with a different but definite order of truth by means of intuition or imagination) is the requirement of concreteness in the work of art — an irreducibility and a novel but wiry outline, as of a neoplatonic or magical symbol, which merely expresses to the sense some truth from the intelligible world. "Like Aristotle, like Goethe after he had read Kant, we desire the concrete, and nothing but the concrete can satisfy us." In these intuitive concrete inventions there is no trace of mechanical pattern, of what Blake might have called 'mathematic form'. Form and matter are coterminous, inseparable; of a detachable meaning there is no trace. In Art, as in the dance, "the body is the soul".

In words like these Wilde concentrates the nineteenth century for the benefit of the twentieth. The Schlegels and Coleridge had developed the thought of the previous century in the direction of that Symbolism which was the nineteenth-century adversary of Realism, by emphasising that the artist imitates *natura naturans*, becoming a power like one of nature's, diffusing through materials "a creative and shaping mind". Art, says A. W. Schlegel, "creating autonomously like nature, both organized and organizing, must form living works, which are first set in motion, not by an outside mechanism like a pendulum, but by an indwelling power like the solar system". We know how much weight the word 'vital' has to bear in the writings of Coleridge. Form is organic (Coleridge distinguishes it from what he calls "shape", or mechanical design) and nature is only the symbolic potential, meaningful only in perception informed by the moral act of imagination. (The meaning of 'moral' here, by the way, is not very remote from what Wilde meant by 'immoral'. If the act of imagination is incorrupt, the product cannot possibly meddle in ethics or have a design upon the reader.) Wilde, in the same spirit, applauded Newman for his observation that Forms are the food of Faith; they are symbols of another order of truth that can never be wholly private because imagination is the shared experience of the race, and they are the prime example of that complete fusion of form and meaning, spirit and body, which also characterises the image of art. Such images the artist is qualified to seek. With stern colour and delicate line he hopes certainly to speak better than he knows; he cannot 'intend' what he says. The image provides its own vigour, and stands free of intention on the one hand and affective considerations on the other; Leonardo's 'intentions' for the Monna Lisa have no more to do with it than Pater's reaction to it. The literary image is not a product of intellect, except in so far as intellect is involved in that creative operation of the whole mind which is Imagination; 'intellect' as such merely contaminates it, attempting to explicate what, to use Bergsonian language, is, though finite, inexplicable, simply because of the way the human mind works.

I have deliberately, in the last paragraph or two, shifted the language from Wildean to Blakean, Coleridgean, Bergsonian, with a hint or two of more immediately fashionable ways of talking about images, because the point is that all make similar assumptions and contribute to the same discussion. A modern poet, Wallace Stevens, who has continued it, has a famous poem about a jar.

47

It took dominion everywhere.
The jar was grey and bare.
It did not give of bird or bush,
Like nothing else in Tennessee.

There has been some dispute about the interpretation of this poem, notably as to whether the poet is *for* Nature or for Art: this is irrelevant, because the point of the jar's *difference*, and the manner of its difference, are what matters. It belongs to a different order of reality, already completely significant and orderly, fixed and immortal. In one sense it is more vital, in another sense less so, than the "slovenly wilderness" around it; the poem itself reconciles opposites by using the jar as a symbol (like the Leech Gatherer) of what moves in stillness, is dead in life, whose meaning and being are the same.

The image I am at present, in a very general way, discussing, is without simple intellectual content, bearing the same relationship to thought as the dancer bears to the dance. As in the dance, there is no disunity of being; "the body is the soul". We might, as I have suggested, use such language of the solitaries of Wordsworth as conveniently as we may of Yeats's dancers and trees; indeed, if we were not so accustomed to think of them as in some way divorced from this tradition, we could apply language of the same sort to nearly all the best poetry of Pound and Eliot. But these images of Yeats have a propriety in the present context which makes them an obvious choice, and in pursuing the icon of the Dancer we shall find ourselves resolving those superficial contradictions of which I spoke earlier. For this Dancer is one of Yeats's great reconciling images, containing life in death, death in life, movement and stillness, action and contemplation, body and soul; in fact all that passionate integrity that was split and destroyed when Descartes, as Yeats puts it, discovered that he could think better in his bed than out of it.

IV

THE DANCER

Her pure and eloquent blood
Spoke in her cheeks, and so distinctly wrought,
That one might almost say, her body thought.
                                              DONNE

Des voluptés intérieures
Le sourire mystérieux. . .

                                              HUGO

Dance is the mother of all languages.
                                              COLLINGWOOD

IN one of his last letters Yeats wrote, "I am happy, and I think full of an energy, an energy I had despaired of. It seems to me that I have found what I wanted. When I try to put it all into a phrase I say, 'Man can embody truth but he cannot know it'. . . The abstract is not life and everywhere draws out its contradictions. You can refute Hegel, but not the Saint or the Song of Sixpence. . ." This is not essentially different from what he might have said as a young man editing Blake. The loathed abstraction was then associated with other names; a new 'system' takes the place of that so carefully studied in the Blake edition, but the quest is the same. How is truth embodied? What concretion, in poetry, takes the place that refutable abstraction occupies in philosophy and other merely intellectual disciplines?

Consider first a very characteristic little vignette from *Discoveries* (1907) called 'The Guitar Player'.

A girl has been playing on the guitar. She is pretty, and if I didn't listen to her I could have watched her, and if I didn't watch her I could have listened. Her voice, the movements of her body, the expression of her face, all said the same thing. . . A movement not of music only but of life came to its perfection. . . The little instrument is quite light, and the player can move freely and express a joy that is not of the fingers and the mind only, but of the whole being; and all the while her movements call up into the mind, so erect and natural she is, whatever is most beautiful in her daily life. . . If you sit at the piano, it is the piano, the mechanism, that is the important thing, and nothing of you means anything but your fingers and your intellect.

This is an early example of that urgent seeking for images to embody beauty defined as non-abstract, as unyielding to philosophers' dichotomies like soul and body; an organic, irreducible beauty, of which female beauty, the beauty of a perfectly proportioned human body, is the type. In the life of the artist, shapelessness and commonness are brought upon the body by the necessary labour of intellect; but it is imperative that this should not be so in the life of a woman. As a companion piece to 'The Guitar Player' Yeats has a passage called 'The Looking Glass', which tells of a girl fresh from school, "with a shrill monotonous voice and an abrupt way of moving"; her education had not been an education of the personality — they had cultivated her memory, not her imagination, and, said, Blake "Imagination has nothing to do with memory". She should have been taught "before all else the heroic discipline of the looking-glass"; but as she was not, she is an emblem of contemporary distraction and division, her body uninformed by grace, her mind abstracted and exhibiting its detachment in her shrill awkwardness. Yeats thanks Verlaine for awakening him to such distinctions as this one between the guitarist and the gauche girl; for of all modern poets Verlaine was the one who most happily defeated abstraction, whose poetry was most clearly a physical presence without separable intellectual content. (He was also the poet who best understood the cost; Yeats speaks of Verlaine's part in teaching him the true nature of the artist's situation, and that "we artists have taken over much to heart that old commandment about seeking after the Kingdom of Heaven".)

Yeats's views on education for girls are, in fact, entirely conditioned by this opinion of the necessity that they should avoid the intellectual labours which would make them shapeless and common and destroy bodily grace. Whenever he speaks on the subject he remembers that, in a way which was important to him, girls are like poems. As early as *Ideas of Good and Evil* (1900) — it is Blake's title, and Blake would probably have approved the contention — he makes this very point in an essay on 'The Symbolism of Poetry'. Complaining of "that brooding over scientific opinion that so often extinguished the central flame in Tennyson", he urges poets to cast out mechanical rhythms (as Verlaine had done), and that approximate diction which will serve for the crudity of mere expressions of opinion; for, he says, "you cannot give a body to something that moves beyond the senses, unless your words are as subtle, as complex, as full of mysterious life, as the body of a flower or of a woman". The remark contains, in germ, Yeats's whole aesthetic; and of course it has implications in the educational field also.

Even earlier, in 1889, Yeats wrote to Katherine Tynan about the delusion that women have anything to do with the higher education and "the great mill called examinations" which men have set up "to destroy the imagination"; if women go through it, "they come out with no repose, no peacefulness, their minds no longer full of secluded paths and umbrage-circled nooks, but loud as chaffering market-places. Mrs. Tod-hunter is a great trouble mostly. She has been thro the mill and has got the noisiest mind I know. She is always denying something". In 1903 he wrote from Bryn Mawr expressing his approval of the teaching there; rich girls were taught to live their lives, whereas in England they were all being turned into teachers. This sounds trivial and light-hearted enough, but it is a recurrent and powerful theme in Yeats's poetry; Constance Markiewitz became an emblem of the woman who barters the rich horn for an old bellows; whose voice grows shrill in argument, whose withered beauty is an image of the politics for which it was blasted. Yeats frankly admitted that he valued the barbarian aristocracy because it highly appreciated activity in men and beauty in women, valuing personal grace and not opinions; and his prayer for his daughter was that she should live in such a milieu and "think opinions are accursed". He would always have agreed with Blake that "careless and gay people are better than those who think"; "it follows, I suppose," says Yeats, "from his praise of life — 'all that lives is holy' — and from his dislike of abstract things". But artists have to think, and are so excluded from full life. Life must include the whole man; "neither Christ nor Buddha nor Socrates wrote a book, for that is to exchange life for a logical process." Yet books are good, and men must write them; but not women; they must think with their bodies.

That most charming and witty poem, 'Michael Robartes and the Dancer', is a serious allusion to this group of ideas.

> Opinion is not worth a rush;
> In this altar-piece the knight,
> Who grips his long spear so to push
> That dragon through the fading light,
> Loved the lady; and it's plain
> The half-dead dragon was her thought,
> That every morning rose again
> And dug its claws and shrieked and fought.
> Could the impossible come to pass
> She would have time to turn her eyes,
> Her lover thought, upon the glass
> And on the instant would grow wise.

The dragon is that abstract thought that threatens the lady's beauty; it is fully emblematic for Yeats, since it stands also for time and multiplicity, those enemies of beauty and repose. The only kind of knowledge truly relevant to the lady is to be achieved in the looking-glass. "May I not put myself to college?" asks the innocent dancer, and she is told of the folly of plucking Athene by the hair:

> For what mere book can grant a knowledge
> With an impassioned gravity
> Appropriate to that beating breast,
> That vigorous thigh, that dreaming eye?
> And may the devil take the rest.

We shall see later why these epithets are significant, why the thigh is expressive and the eye turned inward. The dancer asks:

> And must no beautiful woman be
> Learned like a man?

She is answered in a riddle. The proof that "all must come

to sight and touch" lies in Veronese and "his sacred company"; they "imagined bodies all their days", and Michelangelo proved the intellectual power of mere sinew. All this strikes the girl as heretical; she has "heard said There is great danger in the body"; but to this there is an overwhelming reply:

> Did God in portioning the wine and bread
> Give man his thought or his mere body?

And Robartes goes on to assert

> That blest souls are not composite,
> And that all beautiful women may
> Live in uncomposite blessedness,
> And lead us to the like – if they
> Will banish every thought, unless
> The lineaments that please their view
> When the long looking-glass is full,
> Even to the foot-sole think it too.

"They say such different things at school," sighs the girl.

Robartes' triumphant argument from the Eucharist is, of course, the clinching one; here at any rate the emblem of a thing becomes the thing itself, and a truth of a different order acquires a physical presence, as the Romantic Image must. We are again reminded of Stephen Dedalus, and the Joycean epiphany: "O! In the virgin womb of the imagination the word was made flesh". As for the girl, she too must have no intellectual content that is not appropriate to her form, and expressed by her form; there must be no division of soul and body, but an "uncomposite blessedness".

It is now clear that the lighthearted talk about the education of women is no mere *jeu d'esprit*, but the necessary consequence of a deeper movement of thought, capable of inducing in the poet a permanent passion. In women, as in poems, the body as a whole must be expressive; there should be no question of the mind operating independently of the whole body. In a sense the body does the thinking. Donne's lines on Elizabeth Drury haunted Yeats, as they had haunted poets of the nineteenth century; it should not be surprising that they are still near the tips of critical tongues, and are deeply involved in the twentieth-century mystique of the conceit.

This poem also hints at the strange fact that, for Yeats and others, a whole history of culture is necessary to explain why women and art are no longer thinking bodies. They had been so for a brief period, the period of Unity which Yeats placed in 1450 and the following years. He looks back constantly to Michelangelo, to Veronese and Titian.

> The men that Titian painted, the men that Jongsen painted, even the men of Van Dyck, seemed at moments like great hawks at rest. In the Dublin National Gallery there hung, perhaps still hang, upon the same wall, a portrait of some Venetian gentleman by Strozzi, and Mr. Sargent's painting of President Wilson. Whatever thought broods in the dark eyes of that Venetian gentleman has drawn its life from his whole body; it feeds upon it as the flame feeds upon the candle — and should the thought be changed, his pose would change, his very cloak would rustle for his whole body thinks. President Wilson lives only in the eyes, which are steady and intent; the flesh about the mouth is dead, and the hands are dead, and the clothes suggest no movement of his body nor any movement but that of the valet, who has brushed and folded in mechanical routine.

This is the most impressive statement of an antithesis Yeats is constantly insisting upon; and it has a great part in his "system". Even in Canaletto, he says, there is that power to move us so that "our thought rushes out to the edges of our flesh". But Unity of Being, "using that term as Dante used it when he compared beauty in the *Convito* to a perfectly proportioned human body", has ceased to be possible in life; only in art, and in art of that kind called symbolic, which shuns the mechanical intellect and the dichotomy of form and meaning, can it still be achieved. Even so, it will be achieved only rarely; for modern artists, unlike Donne, linger uneasily between spirit and sense, unable to conquer the notion of their incompatibility, and so attain only a "slight sentimental sensuality which is disagreeable". As it is part of the intention of this essay to indicate the dominant role in much modern poetic thought of the image here emblematized by a woman's body, it is worth saying, in passing, that this view of Donne is the same — allowing for the difference of vocabulary — as that which is still generally accepted; unlike most of the poets who

54

followed him, he achieved poetry in which 'thought' and 'feeling' are identified. To this I shall revert, in the second part of my essay.

The body of a beautiful woman is a constant element in the emblematic equivalents Yeats finds for the symbol, the Romantic Image. Writing, in the 'twenties, of Maud Gonne, he said, "Her face, fused, unified and solitary, the face of some Greek statue, showed little thought, her whole body seemed a masterwork of labouring thought, as though a Scopas had measured and calculated, consorted with Egyptian sages, and mathematicians out of Babylon". Such a remark, with its emphasis on the expressionless face of the Image, introduces the theme in a new guise. *A Vision* provides extensive historical treatment of it. There Yeats makes history accept a pattern which will explain the periodical death of imagination and its symbols, the periodical dissociation of body and spirit. There is, for example, his astonishing comparison between Roman portrait busts, realistic heads screwed on to stock bodies, "heads with world-considering eyes, and bodies... as conventional as the metaphors of a leading article", and "vague Grecian eyes gazing at nothing, Byzantine eyes of drilled ivory staring upon a vision, and those eyelids of China and of India, those veiled or half-veiled eyes weary of world and of vision alike". In Rome, we are told, "the administrative mind, alert attention, had driven out rhythm, exaltation of the body, uncommitted energy"; and those are the qualities of the "riders on the Parthenon". The Roman busts are in the same category as Sargent's Wilson; history moves from periods when the body thinks, and eyes are unseeing of the universe of death, to periods when the body is slack and dull, the eyes consider the world, and the mind is in no significant relation to the whole body. For such unity Yeats looks to Byzantium and the East, as do Hulme and Pound. And here is the germ of an explanation of the fact that the later phases of Romanticism involve a Byzantine revival, and a deepening interest in oriental literature and art. These qualities, possible only when the vision and not the world is the object of man's consideration, are closely associated with definitions of the Image.

It is the object of the artist's long labouring thought, first memorably celebrated by Yeats in 'Adam's Curse', to produce what is passionate and rhythmical, but uncommitted, belonging to the body and not to the abstract intellect: having, in fact — and this is the link between the analogy of the female body and its development, the analogy of the dancer, and the organicist analogy — *a life of its own*. Such a work is independent of the author's intellectual intention; if he comments upon it he is in danger of incurring the odium of the Blakean 'spectre'. What he has to say about it is of no special relevance. (Yeats, like other modern poets, always refused requests for authoritative interpretations of his own work.) Nor has it any one explicable meaning; passion and particular meanings are brought to it. It is the cue for passion, like those statues of the late poem, where girls and boys plant "live lips upon a plummet-measured face". Beauty is the perfectly proportioned body; proportion comes first, passion afterwards. Explication and paraphrase will always fall hopelessly short, simply because they are ways of talking about something other than art, agents of intellect and not of imagination. What matters is the concrete, unique, symbolic object, the living, unified body. *Et tout le reste est littérature.* Upon this body we may press our lips; what we cannot do is to abstract a meaning from it, paraphrase it in terms of our familiar abstractions. In a letter to Sturge Moore, written in 1929, Yeats comments:

> Your definition of beauty was 'the body as it can be imagined as existing in ideal conditions' or some such phrase. I understand it as including all the natural expressions of such a body, its instincts, emotions, etc. Its value is in part that it excludes all that larger modern use of the word and compels us to find another word for the beauty of a mathematic problem or a Cubist picture or of *Mr. Prufrock*. It does not define ideal conditions, nor should it do so, and so it remains a starting point for meditation.

This definition, variously expressed, and without the encumbrance of these fundamentally unnecessary qualifications, served Yeats throughout the forty years of his best poetry, from the moment when he saw what was wrong with his earliest attempts at unifying 'sense' and 'spirit'. "He who sings a lasting song/ Thinks in the marrow bone," and his song defies the dichotomy of body and soul. It has meaning only in terms of its expressive body, like a dancer; or, like a tree, it exists in and for itself, self-begotten (to use a favourite word) because

of its independence of intention, beautiful because perceived
as beautiful.

Together with this definition goes the usual condemnation
of the age which will not accept it. "What is Blake's 'naked
beauty displayed', visible audible wisdom, to the shop-keeping
logicians?" Speaking of an artist whom he certainly admired,
Augustus John, Yeats points out that he is interested in un-
shapeliness, in deviations from the perfect type, without which
there is no 'character'. Of some figures of John he wrote, "A
gymnast would find in all something to amend; and the better
he mended the more would those bodies, as with the voice of
Dürer, declare that ancient canon discovered in the Greek
gymnasium, which, whenever present in painting or sculpture,
shows a compact between the artist and society". He carried
this criterion into life; charmed with the courtly ceremony
that attended the bestowing of his Nobel Prize in Stockholm,
he found the face of Princess Margaretha "full of subtle beauty,
emotional and precise, and impassive with a still intensity
suggesting that final consummate strength which rounds the
spiral of a shell. One finds a similar beauty in wooden busts
taken from Egyptian tombs of the Eighteenth Dynasty..."
And (experienced man of the theatre that he was) he applied
this test to an actress: does her body speak, or only her voice?
Beginners, he says, sometimes

> if told to pick up something, show by the movement of their
> bodies that their idea of doing it is more vivid than the
> doing of it. One gets an impression of thinness in the nature.
> I am watching Miss V — to find out if her inanimate move-
> ments when on the stage come from lack of experience or if
> she has them in life. I watched her sinking into a chair the
> other day to see if her body felt the size and shape of the
> chair before she reached it.

* *

This aristocratic ideal, which links Yeats's theory of history with
the Romantic theory of imagery, applies equally to the beauty
of women and to the beauty of the work of art. Proportion,
movement, meaning, are not intellectual properties, but belong
to that reality of the imagination which is a symbolic reality.
The beauty of a woman, and particularly of a woman in movement, is the emblem of the work of art or Image.

The cult of the speaking body and the face devoid of intellectual meaning — the inward-looking countenance, whether
of drilled eyeball or *sfumato* — assumes in Yeats an extraordinary importance; and when we consider his dancer we
find a symbol both remarkably comprehensive, and with most
interesting antecedents. It was characteristic of him to choose
Pater's passage on Monna Lisa for his *Oxford Book* as the first
of modern poems, lifting it at once out of the stale ecstasies of
'decadent' appreciation, and making it an emblem of both
the *paysage intérieure* and the concreteness of modern poetry;
for this passage has a crucial historical application to which
I shall return. But first let us consider the dancer in more
detail.

She is the image of unified body and soul, the perfect type
of what is called in Yeats's 'system' the Fifteenth Phase, where

> All thought becomes an image, and the soul
> Becomes a body...

"All dreams of the soul," we are told, "end in a beautiful
man's or woman's body." These are the conditions to which
the work of art must approximate; it must attempt to be "separate from everything heterogeneous or casual, from all
character and circumstance, as some Herodiade of our theatre,
dancing seemingly alone in her narrow moving luminous
circle". The bookplate which Sturge Moore was to design for
Yeats's daughter — whose life he desired should resemble, in
ways now clear to us, the Image — was of a dancing girl in the
midst of the sea; the sea is a Blakean emblem of chaos, which
also stands for the modern world in 'A Prayer for my Daughter'. Among other men's poems Yeats chose Joseph Campbell's
'The Dancer' — "In his feet music / On his face death" — and
Turner's poem of the same title, about a girl dancing to a jazz
band with "that strange look, / Unhappy, still, and far away".
One half-expects to find Bridges's 'Eros' — "Surely thy body
is thy mind, / For in thy face is naught to find, / Only thy soft
unchristened smile. . ."; but instead there is William Plomer's
'A Levantine', where there are "Eyes that know all and look
at naught", that indispensable element of the dancer-image
which has to be completed by the notion of wavering, organic
movement. Life sometimes provided an exquisite variation
upon the theme; so with the crazy dance of the girl-poet who

visited Yeats and "stood in desperate music wound", singing
to the sea.

The dancer plays her part in Yeats's system, first as a type
of the Fifteenth Phase, secondly as an element of that sexual
symbolism that grew dominant in his imagery after the 'Supernatural Songs'. A notable poem that ostensibly relates to the
lunar system is 'The Double Vision of Michael Robartes'. It
was written, as Yeats explains, to be a comment upon an early
version of *A Vision*. It is from my purpose here to explain its
esoteric meaning, except to say that the Sphinx is the "intro-
spective knowledge of the mind's self-begotten unity", and the
Buddha "the outward-looking mind". (Yeats confesses an
error concerning the Buddha; he "should have put Christ"
because the instructors told him that Buddha was a Jupiter-
Saturn influence, that is, in the same category as the Sphinx.
As such it appears in 'The Statues'.) These two figures "stand
. . .like heraldic supporters guarding the mystery of the Fifteenth Phase". Between them, emblematic of the mysterious
resolution between outward and inward (aesthetically, this is
the work of Imagination, whether the formulation be Blake's
or Coleridge's or Yeats's) the dancer turns in her narrow
luminous circle, still but moving, dead but alive. She has
"outdanced thought"; concretely visualized, her body silences
the mind; intellect is coterminous with body; or, as Yeats puts
it in words which will recall our ways of talking about the
Donnean conceit, "intellect and emotion. . . are for the
moment one", as they were more usually in the art of the
period 1450-1550, which is "allotted to the gyre of Phase 15".

As usual, when his apparent drift is metaphysical or historical, Yeats's thought is anchored to his conception of the truth-
giving image. The period chosen is not absolutely more important than, say, Henry Adam's choice of 1150-1250 for rather
similar purposes. The point is that the unity of being represented by the dancer, so complete as to be unattainable, is
achieved during some better period, as in the Titians and
Botticellis so much admired by Yeats. (It is mildly surprising
that neither Yeats nor the writers who preceded him in these
paths nor those that have followed him seem to have made
anything of the Botticelli portrait of the dead Giuliano de'
Medici, the perfect image of this life-in-death, and akin to the
mummy, which appealed in slightly different ways to both

Yeats and Wyndham Lewis.) Women and art were, at this
time, speaking bodies. In Yeats's discussion of his Phases 14-16
the treatment of varying degrees of union between the *primary*
and the *antithetical* and so forth is a rationalization (if anything
so obscure might be so called) of much in Yeats's own life; for
it should be remembered that the 15th Phase is a point at
which the doctrines of isolation and Image come together in
the system. This discussion, for example, explains the recurrent
Helen-motif; Maud Gonne was evidently a woman of the
16th Phase, having that excessive beauty which leads to disaster, as Venus chose Vulcan — the kind of beauty from which
he prayed his daughter would be free. Yeats, with his curious
hieratic loaded humour shows us such a woman leading her
man a dance, "a quadrille where all the figures are of their
own composition". This is the irrational independence of the
dancer, her freedom from restraint of time and space, her
visionary concreteness, seen in a slightly different context.
In 'The Double Vision of Michael Robartes' one sees her as
the very heart of Yeats's thinking about poetry and women
(considered as having such powers of self-unification as to become emblematic of the Image). The dancer here reconciles
antithetical movements: the division of soul and body, form
and matter, life and death, artist and audience.

> In contemplation had those three so wrought
> Upon a moment, and so stretched it out,
> That they, time overthrown,
> Were dead, yet flesh and bone.

Although Yeats associated his cult of the inward-looking,
or expressionless face with Blake, it is a recurring feature of
Romantic poetry and painting, and Mario Praz studied it,
more or less under the aspect of Romantic pathology, in his
Romantic Agony. It is, however, important to see it as rather
more than that. Throughout this tradition, the beauty of a
work of art, in which there is no division of form and meaning,
no overplus of 'littérature', is more or less explicitly compared
with the mysterious inexpressive beauty of such women, and
perhaps particularly with that of Salome. The *femme fatale*
is, certainly, the pathological aspect of this Image (we know it
had to have one, because of the emphasis on cost in terms of
life) and in Yeats's Fifteenth Phase the two aspects come

together; but at present it is the aesthetic aspect that interests us.

Praz mentions, as early examples of the *femme fatale*, the Mater Lachrymarum of de Qunicey, the Cleopatra of Gautier, and the Salammbo of Flaubert. Flaubert's version has to a marked degree that withdrawn, virginal quality (in association with cruelty) that became aesthetically important. And it was Flaubert who was so overcome with emotion at the "terrifying stare" of the Sphinx, and described, with all his extraordinary detail, the Egyptian dancers with their expressionless faces. None of this is altogether remote from his concern with the exact representation of the symbolic object. Similarly, the passion of Gautier, and others, for the dance, is not unrelated to their importance in the evolution of the Image. It is impossible to separate the face from the dancer, and the complex of ideas they embody certainly includes some that belong to pathology rather than to aesthetics. But for ease of exposition some pretence of such a separation must be made. For the most part I omit considerations of pathology; and I consider the emblems of expressionless face and dancer in turn.

When an English reader contemplates such faces, he will probably find himself thinking first of Rossetti, a poet admired by Swinburne precisely for his concreteness, for the fulness with which his images realise themselves. In *The Romantic Agony* he is studied in the context of the tradition of algolagnic prostration before a tainted 'Medusean' beauty, and proposed as a source of Pater's Monna Lisa. But looked at from a more aesthetic point of view, Rossetti's Lilith (once divorced from its biographical association with Fanny Cornforth and the vagaries of Rossetti's emotional life) may as well be considered, in Swinburne's phrase, as "a fit raiment for the idea incarnate of faultless fleshly beauty". And this is what Yeats would have understood first. (He does not follow in the way Swinburne points when he compares Lilith with Mademoiselle de Maupin.) When we look from the visual Lilith (where Rossetti has not perhaps quite eliminated all the coarseness of the sitter) to the poem, this is what we find:

> And still she sits, young when the earth is old,
> And, subtly of herself contemplative,
> Draws men to watch the bright web she can weave,
> Till heart and body and life are in its hold.

"Subtly of herself contemplative" — it is the Image, unimpassioned, wise in its whole body, that attracts unbounded passion. The young men who die for it are the true poets and painters of 'Old and New Art'; in the fading world, they turn once more to that true art which is so much more than mere "soulless self-reflections of man's skill", and having had that "luckless luck", as Yeats called it, must suffer, pay the price of that sensibility that enables them to "rend the mist Of devious symbols". To a vigorous man, art in contemplation of itself may seem an inbred business; it is amusing that Yeats's father called Rossetti's art the wrong kind of escape, just as he accused his son of shirking life and concreteness. Yet concreteness of symbol, achieved only by high resolution, is precisely what Rossetti and Yeats alike sought. They stand firm in that tradition: "Lady, I fain could tell how evermore Thy soul I know not from thy body".

Pater's image, as I have said, was a highly significant link in that tradition, as Yeats well understood. The Monna Lisa, of course, owes much to Rossetti — not only to Lilith, but to those sonnets which describe pictures (including one on a Mantegna which strongly recalls Yeats's "thoughtless image of Mantegna's thought"). Rossetti here revives those extravagant glosses, *ut pictura poesis*, on paintings, which Marino had made fashionable two hundred and fifty years earlier — another example of the affinity of certain movements of thought in the nineteenth century for the 'baroque' of Tasso and the Marinisti. Pater's famous lines are in this tradition, but their true importance lies in their adumbration of a complete aesthetic of the Image. Yeats's observations upon it, in defence of his choice of Pater as the first of modern poets, have great interest. According to Yeats, Pater's 'revolutionary' prose-poem — the suggestion is that it is the parent of English *vers libre* — signalled "the revolt against Victorianism", against "irrelevant" (i.e. non-symbolic) natural description, against "the scientific and moral discursiveness" which made Verlaine say of *In Memoriam* that Tennyson, when he should have been broken-hearted, had many reminiscences.

Poets said to one another over their black coffee — a recently imported fashion — 'We must purify poetry of all that is not poetry', and by poetry they meant poetry as it had been written by Catullus, a great name at that time, by the Jacobean writers, by Verlaine, by Baudelaire.

It does not escape Yeats that the poets named here — they might all, incidentally, figure in a list of significant poets drawn up by any but the most recent critic — could have been chosen for the quite different reason that they all have some relevance to the investigation of pathological sexuality. Again the cult of the Image and that of abnormality and estrangement are found in association — as they were, indeed, in the poets who sipped black coffee. Yeats proceeds at once to describe their disastrous lives; this is his generation of drunkards, perverts, madmen with charming manners. But much more important, rhetoric had had its neck wrung. Poetry was being extracted chemically pure, and modern poetry came out of Pater and these, his bitter and gay followers. Yeats affirms this with a rhetorical question in a very obscure section of the Preface to his *Oxford Book*. "Did Pater foreshadow a poetry, a philosophy, where the individual is nothing, the flux of the *Cantos* of Ezra Pound, objects without contour as in *Le Chef d'oeuvre inconnu*, human experience no longer shut into brief lives. . .?" And he professes his admiration for Turner, because he did not forgot, behind the flux, the 'private soul' which is 'the sole source of pain'. It is on this point that he disagrees with Pound, for perfectly clear reasons; the two poets belong to the same tradition, but there is a modern heretical deviation, which Yeats does not accept.

In spite of such disagreements, it is quite satisfactory to speak in a very general way, as Yeats does, about a 'modern' poetry which stems from Pater. The Lady Lisa, says Pater, might be the embodiment of old fancy; she is nevertheless "the symbol of the modern idea", which is "of humanity wrought upon by, and summing up in itself, all modes of thought and life". What is here remarkable is that a female figure with a passionless face can be asked to do so much. And it is not alone in Pater's writing. In the fragment of fictional biography called 'The Child in the House' he dwells upon the aesthetic satisfaction of dead faces — they are absolutely not 'thinking', they are opposed, in their finite and static forms, their concrete but suggestive presences, to what is fluid and abstract.

Hitherto he had never gazed upon dead faces, as sometimes,

63

afterwards, at the *Morgue* in Paris, or in that fair cemetery at Munich, where all the dead must go and lie in state before burial, behind glass windows, among the flowers and incense and holy candles — the aged clergy with their sacred ornaments, the young men in their dancing-shoes and spotless white linen — after which visits, those waxen resistless faces would always live with him for many days, making the broadest sunshine sickly.

This is the simple form of that cult of the dead face which late, separated from all obvious pathological interest, turns up in Yeats, and in Vorticism. It is already surrounded, in a manner which Yeats would find unforgettable, with all the ornaments of ceremony which were for Pater and him alike the essence of religion (see, for example, the poem 'Wisdom'). Pater can write of a room that it "touched him like the face of one dead". At the end of that very odd story, "Emerald Uthwart", a hardened medical man expatiates upon the beauty of the corpse from which he is removing a ball of shot, speaking of "the extreme purity of the outlines, both of face and limbs," and of "the flesh. . . still almost as firm as that of a living person". "This expression of health and life, under my seemingly merciless doings. . . touched me to a degree very unusual in persons of my years and profession. . . The flowers were. . . hastily replaced, the hands and the peak of the handsome nose remaining visible among them; the wind ruffled the fair hair a little; the lips were still red. I shall not forget it". Here is the life-in-death, death-in-life of the Romantic Image, almost essential to the understanding of some of Yeats's poems (and, incidentally, curiously anticipating the tone of Thomas Mann. The beauty of Emerald Uthwart, unimpaired by the shifting distracting motions of life, is a reflection of an aesthetic assumption. The Image has nothing to do with organic life, though it may appear to have; its purity of outline is possible only in a sphere far removed from that in which humanity constantly obtrudes its preoccupations. We look back, once more, to the arbitrary, aniconic, contours of a neoplatonic emblem, and forward to abstraction and the cult of Byzantium. Pater inveighed against the artificial distinction of matter and spirit, and admired Dante and Rossetti alike (as Dante was later to be admired with another companion) for their "delight in

64

concrete definition"; and Rossetti he further admired for his
"chosen type of beauty... whose speech Truth knows not
from her thought, Nor Love her body from her soul". All
these are expressions which, with very little change, might
easily be located in later, and more influential criticism. And
on this point of the paradox of making a dead face stand for
what is most 'vital' in art, Pater provides early types of the
kind of emblem Yeats was later to seek. His interest in it is
reflected in his style; Pater strove always for the 'living' phrase
to embody that "speech of the soul" which all later agreed to
find in Verlaine; yet it is commonplace that Pater wrote
English like a *dead* language, laying out every sentence, as
Max Beerbohm says, "in a shroud".

We may come to a closer understanding of how this kind
of thing struck Yeats and his friends by looking at Arthur
Symons's short book on Pater, late (1932) and rambling
though it is. In it we read, for instance, that Leonardo "created, ambiguously for all the rest of the world, flesh that is flesh
and not flesh, bodies that are bodies and not bodies"; and he
quotes Leonardo's dictum, quite possibly an influential one
for modern literature, that "that figure is not good which does
not express through its gestures the passions of its soul".
Symons dwells upon the Botticelli essay, reminding us that this
painter had not hitherto found a sympathetic English inter-
preter, and emphasising Botticelli's concern for rhythm, his
indifference to what Yeats, pejoratively, calls 'character', so
that the Virgin and Judith and Venus have all alike "in their
eyes the look of those who do or endure great things in a
dream". The famous essay on Giorgione is, for Symons, the
one in which Pater "came perhaps nearer to a complete final
disentangling of the meaning and function of the Arts than any
writer on aesthetics has yet done". He then quotes the second
most famous passage in Pater, on the aspiration of the arts to
the condition of music. In music "the end is not distinct from
the means, the form from the matter, the subject from the
expression; they inhere in and completely saturate each other."
This famous position is, of course, consistent with the aesthetic
of the Image as I have been shadowing it forth. Most, though
not all, the Symbolist poets agreed with Pater; some expressed
a willingness to march to Bayreuth on their knees. Now this is
not a drearily overwrought fancy, an hysterical flight from

commonsense, but the same healthy dread of mathematic form that animated Blake; the same respect for and understanding of the "mighty hot magic" of music that made Coleridge write of Mozart and Beethoven as his kin, as having been "in a state of spirit analogous to mine own when I am at once waiting for, watching, and organically constructing and inwardly constructed by, the *Ideas*, the living Truths, that may be re-excited but cannot be expressed by Words, the Transcendents that give Objectivity to all Objects, the Form to all Images, yet are themselves untranslatable into any Image, unrepresentable by any particular Object. . ." In an altered form it is a dominant assuption in much modern criticism. For Pater, and for Symons, there must be an intense prior meditation by the artist — indeed the quality of the work may be directly dependent upon this — but all the planning and all the intellectual effort must be completely assimilated and distributed in the work, which must not *mean* but *be*. The art that most perfectly achieves this state is music; in poetry there are difficulties of the sort that start barren arguments about the status of the poet's thought extracted and discursively considered; but these are precisely the problems we are continually talking about, and behind all our talk is Pater, with all his apparatus of waxen resistless faces and the one art divinely void of meaning.

The impact of such an aesthetic on Symons and his fellows is, of course, demonstrable in other ways, and its effect is not exclusively to be accounted for in terms of 'art for art's sake'. To admit that would be to confess that the 'tragic generation' merely explored a dead end, and to allow that a completely fresh start had to be made in the early years of the present century. It was not, as we have seen, necessary to agree with Wilde in his total dismissal of the *utile* from art (there are various ways of doing this, some of them, like Kierkegaard's, still having fashonable currency). O'Shaugnessy, for example, certainly held the view of the Image we are discussing; he sought to "carve the marble of pure thought until the thought takes form", and urged his reader not to seek in his work "a sense which is not inherent in the purest Parian". Like the later Imagists he was after the true curve of the Image. But he had nothing to do with art for art's sake, believing, with Coleridge and George Eliot and Pater and Arnold, in their different ways, that the Image had a moral function. When he speaks, rather vaguely perhaps, of "humanity growing" under the influence of perfect forms, he is foreshadowing later solutions of this problem of the *utile*, like, for instance, that of I. A. Richards, who attempted, in *Principles of Literary Criticism*, to establish a quantitative measure of the beneficially affective qualities of poetry. Indeed, this is the central tradition of English Romanticism; the Whistlerian acquiescence in 'decadence', the emphasis upon the work of art as unqualified to impinge upon moral interests, is eccentric. The great modern representative of the central tradition is Yeats, who accepted isolation, but also accepted the duty to communicate beneficially, fortified as he was by a consciousness of the Romantic tenet of the shared symbolic heritage, and tormented at intervals by the fear of a growing privacy, as if the necessary imperfections of the life were on the point of invading perfection of the work — a perfection which certainly entails a morally valuable act of communication.

Whatever may be thought about the *use* of the Image, we may, after this examination of its significance, agree to find the Image itself represented in those mask-like faces of Keats, Rossetti, Pater and Yeats. If they seem inadequate to the task of embodying so elusive an idea, the Dancer will perhaps seem a more perfect emblem of it. I begin with an early treatment of her in this capacity, because it is useful to know the emblem can exist in isolation from its pathological aspect.

Mr. Barker Fairlie has recently, in his study of Heine (1954) drawn attention to that poet's continued interest in the dance. He quoted Heine's words on Franscheska in *Die Bäder von Lucca* — "dancing was her real way of talking" — and more particularly emphasises his report of 'Mme Laurence', a London street-dancer, in *Florentinische Nächte*. "It was not a classical dance, nor a romantic one, nor was there any easy name for it. Mme Laurence was not a great dancer, but she was a natural one, whose body danced, whose face danced. If she held him spellbound, it was not because her outer movements pleased him, but because they seemed to be trying to say something, like words in a special language." What she was saying was tragic; but she became conscious of this only when she was dancing, and forgot about it when she stopped. "Thus the significance of the dance is sustained, and its mystery too: it

speaks, but it only speaks in dance, and cannot be transferred
to any other medium." Heine's dancer, be it noted, is not of
the theatre, certainly not of the ballet; she has a much freer
style, and this suits the Image-dancer better. Many of the later
Romantics — Symons and Yeats among them — shared this
preference, as we shall see. The language of the freely-moving
dancer is more like the Image than the virtuosity of the ballerina's more limited range of movement; Mme Laurence, and
the dancers who filled her place for later poets, is in less danger
of seeming mechanical, her dance is more likely to have form,
the ballerina's often only shape.

But, glad as one is to have this early and simple example, it
must be admitted that the full-blown dancer emblem owes
much to 'decadent' sources, to Huysmans and Wilde, for
example, who derived it partly from Flaubert but mostly from
Gustave Moreau. It is not without interest that Moreau, as
Sr. Praz tells us, imagined himself a disciple of Michelangelo,
so important to Yeats; the Sistine figures are absorbed in
reverie, cut off from movement, achieving a union of intellect
and sense, but also powerfully affective — disturbing, we
recall, to "globe-trotting madam".

Moreau's picture of Salome dancing was a treasured possession of Des Esseintes in *A Rebours*, and Huysmans describes it
in great detail. Before a Herod who sits immobile, like a statue.
"figée dans une pose hiératique de Dieu Hindou", among the
jewels and the perfumes, Salome, "la face recueillie, solennelle,
presque auguste, . . . commence la lubrique danse." This is the
dancer, says Huysmans, "si hantant pour les artistes et les
poètes", yet it is truly accessible "seulement aux cervelles
ébranlées, aiguisées". Her ancestry in Flaubert, and her function as a symbol of the pathological aspect of decadence,
emerge in the description of her as "la déité symbolique de
l'indéstructible Luxure, la déesse de l'immortelle Hystérie, la
Beauté maudite" — the beast, monstrously irresponsible, who
poisons everything she touches, like Helen of old. Huysmans
does not spare effort to make this clear. But she has her other
aspect; and this emerges later in the book as Des Esseintes
contemplates the painting by the dim light of his lamp, with
the *Hérodiade* of Mallarmé open before him.

Invinciblement, il levait les yeux vers elle, la discernait à ses

contours inoubliés, et elle revivait, évoquant sur ses lèvres
ces bizarres et doux vers que Mallarmé lui prête:

> "....   O miroir!
> Eau froide par l'ennui dons ton cadre gelée
> Que de fois, et pendant les heures, desolée
> Des songes et cherchant mes souvenirs qui sont
> Comme des feuilles sous ta glace au trou profond,
> Je m'apparus en toi comme une ombre lointaine!
> Mais, horreur! des soirs, dans ta sévère fontaine,
> J'ai de mon rêve épars connu la nudité!"

Ces vers, il les aimait comme il aimait les oeuvres de ce poète
qui, dans un siècle de suffrage universel et dans un temps de
lucre, vivait à l'écart des lettres, abrité de la sottise environ-
nante par son dédain, se complaisant, loin du monde, aux
surprises de l'intellect, aux visions de sa cervelle, raffinant
sur des pensées déjà spécieuses, les greffant de finesses byzan-
tines, les perpétuant en des déductions légèrement indi-
quées que reliait à peine un imperceptible fil. . .
Percevant les analogies les plus lointaines, il désignait sou-
vent d'une terme donnant à la fois, par un effet de simili-
tude, la forme, le parfum, la couleur, la qualité, l'éclat,
l'objet ou l'être auquel il eût fallu accoler de nombreuses et
de différentes épithètes pour en dégager toutes les faces,
toutes les nuances, s'il avait été simplement indiqué par son
nom technique. Il parvenait ainsi à abolir l'énonce de la
comparaison qui s'établissait, toute seule, dans l'esprit du
lecteur, par l'analogie, dès qu'il avait pénétré le symbole, et
il se dispensait d'éparpiller l'attention sur chacune des
qualités qu'auraient pu présenter, un à un, les adjectifs
placés à la queue leu-leu, la concentrait sur un seul mot, sur
un tout, produisant, comme pour un tableau par exemple,
un aspect unique et complet, un ensemble.

The tone of the first paragraph of Huysmans' comment on
the verses is by now familiar; the second is, as it were, a concise
manifesto of Symbolism. By this juxtaposition the Dancer becomes an emblem with a double aspect. Previously Mallarmé's
poem, begun about 1864, had not had much celebrity, and it
was partly the success of Huysmans' allusion to it that gave
Mallarmé, the most subtle of Symbolist aestheticians, his

wider fame. What Huysmans does is to correlate the pathological and aesthetic aspects of the Dancer motif. Intellectual and
physical isolation are easily represented by diseases which are
the consequences of uncontrolled feeling; and when this becomes the artist's preferred subject he evolves the Herodiade
emblem, representing at once the cruelty of the isolation and
the beauty (distinct from life yet vital) of its product.

We have now to think first of dancers in general, as emblem-
atically used; and then of Salome in particular. The general
theme is used in an extraordinary variety of ways; and with
varying degrees of respectability. At one end of the scale we
find Mallarmé's use of the Dancer to represent a central and
inexpressible aesthetic idea; at the other the English intellectual's cult of the music hall. Symons himself, always at the
centre of his period and herald of its successor, was a devotee
of dancing, and was often at the Alhambra, looking for the
sort of sensation Jane Avril was providing in Paris. His poem
'To a Dancer' talks about "her body's melody", and the better
one called 'Javanese Dancers' contains these lines:

> Smiling between her painted lids a smile,
> Motionless, unintelligible, she twines
> Her fingers into mazy lines;
> The scarves across her fingers twine the while...
>
> Still, with fixed eyes, monotonously still,
> Mysteriously, with smiles inanimate,
> With lingering feet that undulate,
> With sinuous fingers, spectral hands that thrill...

And in 'La Mélinite: Moulin Rouge' he speaks of Jane
Avril herself in these terms:

> Alone, apart, one dancer watches
> Her mirrored, morbid grace;
> Before the mirror, face to face,
> Alone she watches
> Her morbid, vague, ambiguous grace...
>
> And, enigmatically smiling,
> In the mysterious night,
> She dances for her own delight,
> A shadow smiling
> Back to a shadow in the night.

70

This is Toulouse-Lautrec's Jane Avril. She was a music-hall dancer with a circus background, and her dancing, like that of Heine's Mme Laurence, belonged to no particular genre. She moved, it is said, with remarkable plasticity, her face an ecstatic mask, in a dance she herself designed, or merely improvised. She had many imitators, but no rivals, and achieved great celebrity among poets and painters, who admired the freedom, the 'significant form' of her dance, as well as her strange personal attractions. She had in repose a solemn and withdrawn expression, which Toulouse-Lautrec makes more mysterious and gloomy than it probably was. Such poems as this of Symons, though of course they do not contain 'doctrine', take the whole ambiance of such dancers for granted; and we may be sure that behind these rather *louche* manifestations there is some such theory as that of Mallarmé, for whom, at one period, the dancer was the emblem of identical form and meaning, "l'incorporation visuelle de l'idée". The Dance signified the artist's effort "à vêtir l'idée d'une forme sensible"; we should remember that 'l'idée' is here used in a limited sense, meaning a truth inaccessible to unaided intellect. Mallarmé wrote a long study of Loïe Fuller, an American dancer who exploited, in the Paris of this period, a new taste for unconventional dancing. She performed at the Folies Bergères, in a great whirl of shining draperies, the scope of which she extended by manipulating sticks (the effect is illustrated by Toulouse-Lautrec). "Au bain terrible des étoffes se pâme, radieuse, froide, la figurante qui illustre maint thême giratoire où tend une trame loin épanouie, pétale et papillon géants, déferlement, tout d'ordre net et élémentaire... Or cette transition de sonorités aux tissus... est uniquement le sortilège qu'opère la Loïe Fuller, par instinct, avec l'exagération, les retraits, de jupe ou d'aile, instituant un lieu. L'enchanteresse fait l'ambiance, la tire de soi et l'y rentre, par un silence palpité de crêpes de chine." Mallarmé finds this much superior to the conventional ballet; there is no insipid scenery, the dancer constitutes the whole image. So, he says, though he cannot describe adequately this "éclosion contemporaine", he cannot let it pass without comment, for it has more than local significance. Finally he commends an observation of Rodenbach's, that the task of the performer is to enrich by every kind of insubstantial ('vaporeux') adornment the enchantment of dances *"où leur corps n'apparaît que comme le rhythme d'où tout dépend mais qui le cache"*. He speaks of the dancer exactly as he does of poetry.

That Symons thought along these same lines is evident. If we had no direct proof we could argue that his whole aesthetic tends in this direction, that his mind works like this. For example, in his *Spiritual Adventures* (1905) — an unjustly neglected book — there is the story of 'Esther Kahn', about a Jewish actress (her eyes "intolerably ambiguous without intention") who achieves mastery in her art only when she becomes the mindless vehicle of tragedy; and this at the expense of personal happiness. His musician, Christian Trevalga, knows by instinct that music is free of "expressible meaning", and as he moves into the isolation of madness he hears it "like pure joy, speaking its own language". "When the angels talk among themselves," he wrote, "their speech is art; for they do not talk as men do, to discuss matters or to relate facts, but to express either love or wisdom." This is the old distinction that Coleridge illustrated from Milton; it serves in defence of the Romantic theory of the Image as anti-discursive; and the Dancer represents just that. Inevitably, for Symons also, the thory has its 'decadent' aspect; so the painter, Peter Waydelin, applies his Baudelairian love of cosmetics to a study of the blank-faced women in Japanese paintings, and the deformed mistress appears as the Baroness von Eckstein, whose face was scarred by vitriol, in the remarkable 'Journal of Henry Luxulyan'. Women, for this neurotic diarist, are contemptible except in so far as they are mysterious, and mysterious in that they transcend discourse.

I have glanced at Symons's fiction simply to make the point that most of the elements of that attitude which is preliminary to the cult of the Dancer exist, and are habitually given expression, in his work, even when he is not theorizing. When he was, he was capable of providing a perfectly clear expression of the dancer's relation to this complex of ideas, as may be seen from an essay he contributed to *The Dome* in 1898. This is in fact the fullest treatment I know of what may be called the *topos* of the Dancer; and the dance finally takes the place of music in the Paterian formula. The essay is called 'Ballet, Pantomime and Poetic Drama', and its first section is 'The World as Ballet'. In it he says of the dance that "the avoidance of emphasis, the evasive, winding turn of things; and above all. *the intellectual as well as sensuous appeal of a living symbol*, which can but reach the brain through the eyes, in the visual, concrete, imaginative way; has seemed to make the ballet concentrate in itself a good deal of the modern ideal in matters of artistic expression. *Nothing is stated*, there is no intrusion of words used for the *irrelevant purpose of describing*. . . and the dancer, with her gesture, *all pure symbol*, evokes, from her mere beautiful motion, idea, sensation, all that one need ever to know of event". Here Symons is transferring the terms appropriate to the Romantic Image to the dancer; I have italicised some of the more striking examples of this. It is the dancer's movement (contrasted with the immobility of sculpture) and the fact that this movement is passionate, controlled not by intellect but by rhythm and the demands of plastic form, that make her an emblem of joy (Symons uses the word) and give her a fantastic reality, a form above life, so that she becomes a complete representation of the Image.

But the Image is never for long dissociated from the consideration of its cost; and to see how the dancer contrives to emblematize this also we must return to the figure of Salome, whom we have already mentioned in connexion with the influence of Moreau and Huysmans on later poets. Salome is the Dancer in the special role of the Image that costs the artist personal happiness, indeed life itself. She had a great vogue, and the brief account I give of her is of a curiously complicated subject.

When Richard Strauss heard Elisabeth Schumann sing, he expressed a great desire to hear her in the role of Salome; and when she protested the apparently obvious unsuitability of her voice, he explained that what the part needed was not some heroic soprano (which is in fact what we usually get) but precisely the transparent, even girlish, clarity of her tone. Unhappily nothing came of the proposal, but it seems clear that Strauss was not talking eccentrically, and that he had recognized in Mme Schumann's voice the possibility of her achieving some vocal equivalent for that unemotional, disengaged quality — Yeats's word might be 'uncommitted' — which Wilde gave his Salome, and which, despite the ridicule of critics, was fundamental to his conception of her. There should be an innocent, totally destructive malice; beauty inhumanly immature and careless cruelty. This is the type.

The English Herodiades occasionally degenerate into mere demonstrations of the dancer's pathological aspect, as in the extraordinary fancy of Evan John, who makes Salome clutch the Baptist's severed head between her thighs. The more characteristic form is found in O'Shaugnessy's 'The Daughter of Herodias', where Salome dances

> A certain measure that was like some spell
> Of winding magic, wherein heaven and hell
> Were joined to kill men's souls eternally
> In some mid ecstasy. . .
> And through the blazing of the numberless
> And whirling jewelled fires of her dress,
> Her perfect face no passion could disarm
> Of its reposeful charm.

Here we are once more near the Salome of Wilde, and the dancer-image which certainly affected Yeats. It seems probable that not only Salome, but other Wildean figures like Helen and the Sphinx influenced him. Wilde's Helen is like Yeats's before the purification of motive, so to speak, induced by association with Maud Gonne, and the annunciatory imagery Yeats later attached to it. His Sphinx (which had associations with both Ricketts and Beardsley, both much admired by Yeats) has the "curved archaic smile" upon which the later poet speculated so much, as well as all the apparatus of secret contemplation and the power to evoke monstrous passion. Wilde's Salome is Moreau's writ large, though not without irony; and, as Sr. Praz has shown, he owed something to Flaubert, whose Salome forgets the name of the man whose head she is dancing for, and to Maeterlinck, who taught him to make Salome a childish character. But he added to Salome what had not been hers before — cruelty and desire, passions which had formerly been her mother's: "C'est pour mon propre plaisir que je demande la tête. . ." This has importance for Yeats.

In Yeats's work, the notion of human sacrifice as the price of the symbolic dance is deeply and curiously embedded. From very early days he associates Salome with the Sidhe. 'The Hosting of the Sidhe' is the first poem in *The Wind Among the Reeds* (1899):

Empty your heart of its mortal dream,
The winds awaken, the leaves whirl round,
Our cheeks are pale, our hair is unbound,
Our breasts are heaving, our eyes are agleam,
Our arms are waving, our lips are apart;
And if any gaze on our rushing band,
We come between him and the deed of his hand,
We come between him and the hope of his heart.

In his own comment on this poem Yeats explains that "the gods of ancient Ireland", under various titles including 'the Sidhe', "still ride the country as of old. Sidhe is also Gaelic for wind, and certainly the Sidhe have much to do with the wind. They journey in whirling wind, the winds that were called the dance of the daughters of Herodias in the Middle Ages, Herodias doubtless taking the place of some old goddess". There is here a somewhat complex association of ideas — the Irish fairies whose 'touch' Yeats associates with the 'marking' or damnation of a poet with the vortex of the whirlwind and with the daughter of Herodias. For this last, Yeats is apparently drawing upon some legend like that of the goblin-hunt, such as that in Heine's 'Atta Troll', for in this hunt Herodias herself travels. However the association came about, the contamination of Salome by fairies persisted in Yeats's mind, and, appearing from time to time, burst out flourishing in the last years, when he dwelt much upon his own mythologies. So, in the passage I have already quoted from *The Tragic Generation*, he speaks of his art as, "separate from everything heterogeneous and casual, from all character and circumstance, as some Herodiade of our theatre, dancing seemingly alone in her narrow luminous circle." Here she is, quite clearly, an emblem of the perfect work of art. In the easy transit to his theories of personality and history, she becomes the Fifteenth Phase, perfect unity of being, with the moon at the full. For Yeats is certainly thinking of Salome — though a Salome stripped of all the 'decadent' trappings she has in Moreau and Wilde — when he writes of the dancing girl in the vision at Cashel. Salome can even be, for Yeats, the symbol of the moment of cultural equilibrium preceding the Christian revelation and the great 'antithetical' phase of Christian dominance, the end of the full heroic life.

75

When I think of the moment before revelation I think of Salome — she, too, delicately tinted, or maybe mahogany dark — dancing before Herod and receiving the Prophet's head in her indifferent hands, and wonder if what seems to us decadence was not in reality the exaltation of the muscular flesh and of civilisation perfectly achieved.

And this is not the only connection between Salome and the 'system'. Sometimes the link is provided by the host of the Sidhe, as in the concluding poem of 'Nineteen Hundred and Nineteen' — "evil gathers head, Herodias' daughters have returned again" — where she again signifies a complete historical change of direction. In the second poem of the same sequence the whirling dancer images the Great Year itself.

These are historical significations closely related to the aesthetic values of the same figure. It is hardly too much to say that whenever Yeats refers back to the historical concept of unity of being, or to the aesthetic one of beauty as a perfectly proportioned human body, the image of Salome is likely to occur to him; a test case might be the famous passage on Byzantium in *A Vision*, when he says he would, of all periods, choose to live for a month in Byzantium "a little before Justinian opened St. Sophia and closed the Academy of Plato"; he would, he says, seek out "some philosophical worker in mosaic who could answer all my questions, the supernatural descending nearer to him than to Plotinus even, for the pride of his delicate skill would make what was an instrument of power to princes and clerics, a murderous madness in the mob, show as a lovely flexible presence like that of a perfect human body". We know what the other characteristics of this perfect body must be; the face without intellectual disturbance, the meaning fully incarnate, no intrusive 'character', for so long as the dance lasts the dancer cannot be distinguished from it. Yeats finds more personal applications; in a diary of 1930 he wrote that illness and age, leaving their marks on his face, might have changed his character, but not his poetry. "My character is so little myself that all my life it has thwarted me. It has affected my poems, my true self, no more than the character of a dancer affects the movements of a dance". The distinction is familiar enough; it is the old one of self and anti-self, face and mask, involving the dilemma of action and

76

contemplation. But the presence of the dancer in the metaphor gives it a wider significance; Salome is the mask in action, the image independent of thought and thinker. She is the work of art in all its relations, dancing not only on "our stage", but in "the predestined dancing-place" of Tir n'an Ogue, the Paradise known to Oisin, where they "mock at Death and Time", and upon the dancing floor of Byzantium, and in that sexual dance which is an earthly copy of some divine Herodian movement.

If we remember these rich complexities of attitude, it will not surprise us that Yeats's discovery of the Japanese Nō plays was an important moment in his career. They were to him what Wagner was to the French. Much of his earlier thought on the drama must have seemed to him a steady, though unwitting, progress in the direction of the Nō; he almost invented it himself. Take, for example, his essay on 'The Tragic Theatre' (1910). Character, he says, has nothing to do with tragedy; tragedy is like that youthful beauty which is devoid of character, for character "grows with time, like the ash of a burning stick". The true poetical art is that of Hamlet's "Absent thee from felicity awhile", quite characterless; or of Titian's portrait of Ariosto, where the face is "like some vessel soon to be full of wine".

> . . .if we are painters, we shall express personal emotion through ideal form, a symbolism handled by the generations, a mask from whose eyes the disembodied looks, a style that remembers many masters, that it may escape contemporary suggestion; or we shall leave out some element of reality as in Byzantine painting, where there is no mass, nothing in relief; and so it is that in the supreme moment of tragic art there comes upon one that strange sensation as though the hair of one's head stood up. And when we love, if it be in the excitement of youth, do we not also, that the flood may find no stone to convulse, no wall to narrow it, exclude character or the signs of it by choosing that beauty which seems unearthly because the individual woman is lost amid the labyrinth of its lines as though life were trembling into stillness and silence, or at last folding itself away?

Here the lack of character and disembodied intellect in the woman, the invocation of Byzantium, have more to do with the pure presentation of the image in the theatre than with the misty, 'ninetyish unwordliness which is the first response the passage strikes in the modern mind; realism was the proper enemy of a movement more serious than a merely fashionable 'decadence'. The girl's lack of character, the 'emptiness' of Ariosto's face, are the emblems of the tragic art Yeats wants for the theatre. In practical terms it meant masks; it meant "rhythm, balance, pattern, images that remind us of vast patterns". It meant music. What in fact was needed was a drama very like the Nō.

Yeats was introduced to the Japanese Nō by Ezra Pound, who was translating examples with the help of Ernest Fenellosa. He saw the relation to his own work, and of course admired the plays as the work of dedicated artists done for a class of cultivated warrior-aristocrats — this was for Yeats the true heroic situation for poetry, life being all action and courtesy, poetry all contemplation and style. The Japanese poet-actors of the Nō tradition, stored up in the *Kwadenshō* of Sēami, spent their lives, and indeed their souls, freely in the service of an exquisite art. Everything Yeats could discover about the plays confirmed him in opinions long held. There is in them an overwhelming concern that every detail of text, dance and presentation shall be perfectly controlled; and to this concern the life of the poet, which as a man he would desire to be perfect in order to escape rebirth, must be sacrificed. "These matchless arts of dance and song," laments Seami, "have laid too strong, oh all too strong, a hold upon an old man's heart! They have become a stumbling-block in his path to salvation." Acting and dancing were conventional, and the doctrine of imitation was one Yeats must have found congenial. There should be no straining after realism.

In imitation there shoulds be a tinge of the "unlike". For if imitation be pressed too far it impinges on reality and ceases to give an impression of likeness. If one aims only at the beautiful, the "flower" is sure to appear... The appearance of old age will often be best given by making all movements a little late, so that they come just after the musical beat. If the actor bears this is mind, he may be as lively and energetic as he pleases. For in old age the limbs are heavy and the ears slow; there is the will to move but not the corresponding capacity. . . . If, because the actor has noticed that old men walk with bent knees and back, and have shrunken frames, he simply imitates these characteristics, he may achieve an appearance of decrepitude, but it will be on the expense of the "flower". And if the "flower" be lacking there will be no beauty in his impersonation.

The "flower", *yūgen*, is the untranslatable symbol of the joy that comes with a perfectly achieved beauty. In his essay, 'Certain Noble Plays of Japan', written for Pound's collection, Yeats repeats a story to this purpose.

A young man was following a stately old woman through the streets of a Japanese town, and presently she turned to him and spoke: "Why do you follow me?" "Because you are so interesting." "That is not so, I am too old to be interest-'ing." But he wished, he told her, to become a player of old women on the Noh stage. "If he would become famous as a Noh player, she said, he must not observe life, nor put on an old voice and stint the music of his voice. He must know how to suggest an old woman and yet find it all in the heart."

Every aspect of the technique and presentation of Nō must have struck Yeats as certain proof of the soundness of his own theory of drama, which in itself stems from the Romantic Image. Above all these were dance-plays, and so antithetical to the realism that was, in Yeats's view, draining the force of the theatre, so hostile indeed to the whole mimetic tradition of the West, that the players went masked. The Nō answered, better than Wagner or any merely synaesthetic experiment, the prayer of a Symbolist poet for a fitting theatre — Mallarmé has desired a Symbolist drama, but was put off by the prospect of irrelevant *expression* in the actor's faces — and though they came too late to coincide with Yeats's earlier mood of heroic vision they provided him with a dramatic medium in which he at last fully found himself as a poet for the theatre. They provided him with the means of dealing with mythological-religious themes in a theatre where character was abolished by the mask, and musical movement, the symbolic order of art, superseded the fragmentary passion of the speaking voice and the naturalism of modern stage movement. His actors would have the blank, inward faces of the wooden Japanese masks; they would not necessarily even speak their own lines. Musicians would frame the action, and comment in song. All would be inexplicit, suggestive, but faultless in design; and often the climax of the play would be a dance like Salome's. There would be no separable meaning; the verses would be spoken as the dance was danced, and would dispense with that kind of expression that points 'meaning'.

The first of the dance-plays came only a year after 'Certain Noble Plays of Japan'. It was *At The Hawk's Well*. In it the young Cuchulain, like the old man, is cursed for his dealings with the 'dancers', with the Woman of the Sidhe. Already the dance-play begins to be associated with Salome, though at several removes. Two years later, in *The Only Jealousy of Emer*, the deserted Emer complains of the same Woman:

> I know her sort.
> They find our men asleep, weary with war,
> Lap them in cloudy hair or kiss their lips;
> Our men awake in ignorance of it all
> But when we take them in our arms at night
> We cannot break their solitude.

This Woman is masked, and in appearance and movement inhuman. It is in the last plays that the Salome of the Sidhe appears in full panoply. In *A Full Moon in March* (1935) a queen is to be won by him who sings his passion best. The candidate presented in a swineherd, foul and ugly, and wearing a "half-savage mask".

> Queen, look at me, look long at these foul rags,
> At hair more foul and ragged than my rags;
> Look on my scratched foul flesh. Have I not come
> Through dust and mire? There in the dust and mire
> Beasts scratched my flesh; my memory too is gone,
> Because great solitudes have driven me mad.
> But when I look into a stream, the face
> That trembles upon the surface makes me think
> My origin more foul than rag or flesh.

He is, of course, the accursed singer, seeking his prize. The Queen is his prize, "crueller than solitude, Forest or beast".

> Some I have killed or maimed
> Because their singing put me in a rage,
> And some because they came at all. Men hold
> That woman's beauty is a kindly thing,
> But they that call me cruel speak the truth,
> Cruel as the winter of virginity.

Her "woman's beauty" is the Image; and the speech is of its cost. The Queen is insulted by the appearance of the swineherd; she has him beheaded, and dances before his severed head, having laid it upon the throne. The head sings. The poem is related to the 'system', and in fact ends with a passage of astonishing power that represents the Queen as the Fifteenth Phase, complete, lacking in the fury and the mire; yet in another sense incomplete, *because* lacking the destructive passions of the flesh; but even in this capacity, as we have seen, she continues to represent the Image (the relation of which to the fury and the mire will shortly concern us) and she is clearly derived from Salome, the whim that cost John his head, and the whole complex of isolated poet and the symbol that mitigates his remorse. *The King of the Great Clock Tower* (1935) has the same central situation. Its opening words relate the theme to that of the dancing paradise — "They dance all day that dance in Tir-nan-oge". The Queen wears "a beautiful impassive mask" and is silent, having nothing to do with the King of Time (the Image being free of time and intellect). A Stroller enters in "a wild halfsavage mask", having sworn to see the Queen he had put into his songs (the application in the present context needs no labouring) and having been promised by Aengus, God of Love, that she would dance for him and kiss his mouth. His head is cut off and placed on the throne; the Queen dances, takes the head upon her shoulder; it sings of the more than sexual joys of eternity. She kisses it on the stroke of midnight (the point at which it is easiest to imagine time away). The King moves to kill her, but lays the sword at her feet (her nature conquers Time). The singers celebrate the perpetual dance, the type of earthly beauty, in Tir-nan-Oge. This play is primarily related to the hermetic speculations of the 'Supernatural Songs', but the old equivalences still obtain. The Stroller is the Artist and the Queen is the Image, out of time and deathless, speaking no intellectual language. "It was more original than Yeats thought," says Hone, "for upon referring to *Salome* he found that Wilde's dance was never danced with the head in her hands." After this it is impossible to doubt the reality of the relationship existing for Yeats between Salome and the Image.

Yeats's next play was the brilliant *Herne's Egg* (1938), only obliquely related to this theme; and then came his last plays, *Purgatory* and *The Death of Cuchulain* (1939), perhaps his finest. "I promise a dance", says the Old Man in the Prologue to the last play.

> I wanted a dance, because where there are no words there is less to spoil. Emer must dance, there must be severed heads — I am old, I belong to mythology — severed heads for her to dance before. I had thought to have had those heads carved, but no, if the dancer can dance properly no wood-carving can look as well as a parallelogram of painted wood. But I was at my wit's end to find a good dancer; I could have got such a dancer once, but she has gone; the tragi-comedian dancer, the tragic dancer, upon the same neck love and loathing, life and death. I spit three times. I spit upon the dancers painted by Degas. I spit upon their short bodices, their stiff stays, their toes whereon they spin like pegtops, above all upon that chambermaid face. They might have looked timeless, Rameses the Great, but not the chambermaid, that old maid history. I spit! I spit! I spit!

Emer does dance before the severed head of Cuchulain, a mere black parallelogram, and is about to prostrate herself before it when she hears the faint bird-notes of his departing spirit. This superb play has a deliberate quality of personal allegory which must always dominate our interests; further, the Salome-figure has (very naturally, since for Yeats as for Blake eschatology was a branch of aesthetics) been taken up into the predominantly eschatological pattern of the poet's later thought. But its relevance to the Dancer, as we have here considered it, is none the less clear; the dancer of the play is loved and loathed, timeless: and "there must be severed heads". The expressionless mask has developed into a featureless black block of wood. The poet-hero escapes at last.

I come now, having commented on some of Yeats's other

dancers, to the poem in which the Dancer makes her most remarkable appearance. 'Among Schoolchildren' is the work of a mind which is itself a system of symbolic correspondences, self-exciting, difficult because the particularities are not shared by the reader — but his interests are not properly in the mind but in the product, which is the sort of poetry that instantly registers itself as of the best. What I have to say of the poem should not be read as an attempt to provide another explication of it, or to provide a psychological contribution to the understanding of the poet. I have, as the preceding pages show, a rather narrow interest in its images, and that is what I propose to pursue.

The "sixty-year-old smiling public man" of the poem is caught in the act of approving, because he has ventured out of his *genre*, of a way of educating children which, as we have seen, is completely inimical to his profoundest convictions. The tone is of self-mockery, gentle and indeed somewhat mincing, with a hint of unambitious irony — "in the best modern way", we can pick up this note without prior information, but it is at any rate interesting to know that the children are engaged in the wrong labour, the antithesis of the heroic labour of the looking-glass. The old man, because he is old and a *public* man, does not protest, but sees himself as amusingly humiliated, not too seriously betrayed, putting up with the shapelessness and commonness that life has visited upon him. But children of the kind he sees before him remind him of the great image of a lady who was all they could not hope to be, a daughter of imagination, not of memory; a daughter of the swan, the perfect emblem of the soul, and like Leda the sign of an annunciation of paganism and heroic poetry, for which the soul is well-lost. But she too is old; he thinks of her present image: "Did Quattrocento finger fashion it?" For even in old age she has that quality of the speaking body, the intransigent vision, perhaps, of Mantegna. And he himself had had beauty, though he had spent it in his isolation and intellectual effort, and become shapeless and common, the old scarecrow of the later poems. The fifth stanza develops this theme, the destruction of the body by Adam's curse, which for Yeats is the curse of labour. It is a reworking of some lines from *At The Hawk's Well*, of ten years earlier.

A mother that saw her son
Doubled over with speckled shin,
Cross-grained with ninety years,
Would cry, 'How little worth
Were all my hopes and fears
And the hard pain of his birth!'

This old man has lain in wait for fifty years, but he "is one whom the dancers cheat"; "wisdom," conclude the singers, "must lead a bitter life," and he who pursues it prizes the dry stones of a well and the leafless tree above a comfortable door and an old hearth, children and the indolent meadows. This is the plight of the old man in the schoolroom, to be with the scarecrow thinkers and teachers and poets, out of life; the scarecrow is the emblem of such a man, because he is a absurd, rigid diagram of living flesh that would break the heart of the woman who suffered the pang of his birth.

But there are other heartbreakers, though these do not change with time, but "keep a marble or a bronze repose". 'Marble and bronze' is a recurrent minor motive in Yeats. It occurs in simple form in 'The Living Beauty' (1919), where there is an antithetical relationship between it and that which is truly 'alive' — alive in the normal sense, and possessing that speaking body which includes the soul.

I bade, because the wick and oil are spent,
And frozen are the channels of the blood,
My discontented heart to draw content
From beauty that is cast out of a mould
In bronze, or that in dazzling marble appears,
Appears, but when we have gone is gone again,
Being more indifferent to our solitude
Than 'twere an apparition. O heart, we are old;
The living beauty is for younger men:
We cannot pay its tribute of wild tears.

These masterly verses have the seeds of much later poetry. The purpose of art, in the life of the poet, is to mitigate isolation by providing the Image which is the daily victory. "I suffered continual remorse, and only became content when my abstractions had composed themselves into picture and dramatisation. . ." But the relief is impermanent; the poet discovers that "he has made, after the manner of his kind, Mere images".

There is a tormenting contrast between the images (signified by the bronze and marble statuettes) and the living beauty. And out of this contrast grows the need for a poetic image which will resemble the living beauty rather than the marble or bronze. No static image will now serve; there must be movement, the different sort of life that a dancer has by comparison with the most perfect object of art. Here we see, in strictly poetic terms, a change comparable to that wrought by Pound in the abandonment of Imagism, and the development of a dynamic image-theory. The Image is to be all movement, yet with a kind of stillness. She lacks separable intellectual content, her meanings, as the intellect receives them, must constantly be changing. She has the impassive, characterless face of Salome, so that there is nothing but the dance, and she and the dance are inconceivable apart, indivisible as body and soul, meaning and form, ought to be. The Dancer, in fact is, in Yeats's favourite expression, 'self-begotten', independent of labour; as such she differs totally from the artist who seeks her. She can exist only in the predestined dancing-place, where, free from Adam's curse, beauty is born of itself, without the labour of childbirth or the labour of art; where art means wholly what it *is*. The tree also means what it is, and its beauty is a function of its whole being, achieved without cost, causing no ugliness in an artist. This is one of the senses of the magnificent concluding stanza:

> Labour is blossoming or dancing where
> The body is not bruised to pleasure soul,
> Nor beauty born out of its own despair,
> Nor blear-eyed wisdom out of midnight oil.
> O chestnut tree, great-rooted blossomer,
> Are you the leaf, the blossom or the bole?
> O body swayed to music, O brightening glance,
> How can we know the dancer from the dance?

"A savoir que la danseuse *n'est pas une femme qui danse*, pour ces motifs juxtaposés qu'elle *n'est pas une femme*, mais un métaphore résumant un des aspects élémentaires de notre forme, glaive, coupe, fleur, etc., et *qu'elle ne danse pas*, suggérant, par le prodige de raccourcis ou d'eláns, avec une écriture corporelle ce qu'il faudrait des paragraphes en prose dialoguée autant que déscriptive, pour exprimer, dans la rédaction: *poème dégagé de tout appareil du scribe.*" This is Mallarmé's accurate prediction of Yeats's poem.

'Among Schoolchildren' might well be treated as the central statement of the whole complex position of isolation and the Image. Later there were many fine poems that dealt with the nature of the sacrifice, and of the fugitive victory; like 'Vacillation', which asks the question "What is joy?" and answers it with an image, of a sort to be achieved only by choosing the way of Homer and shunning salvation; or like the 'Dialogue of Self and Soul', or the simple statements of 'The Choice':

> The intellect of man is forced to choose
> Perfection of the life or of the work,
> And if it choose the second must refuse
> A heavenly mansion, raging in the dark.
>
> When all the story's finished, what's the news?
> In luck or out the toil has left its mark:
> That old perplexity an empty purse,
> Or the day's vanity, the night's remorse.

There are poems, too, which give the problem a more specifically religious turn. The paradise in which labour and beauty are one, where beauty is self-begotten and costs nothing, is the artificial paradise of a poet deeply disturbed by the cost in labour. The ambiguities of hatred and love for 'marble and bronze' inform not only those poems in which Yeats praises the active aristocratic life and its courtesies, but also the Byzantium poems, which also celebrate the paradisal end of the dilemma. In this paradise life, all those delighting manifestations of growth and change in which the scarecrow has forfeited his part, give way to a new condition in which marble and bronze are the true life and inhabit a changeless world, beyond time and intellect (become, indeed, the image truly conceived, without human considerations of cost). The artist himself may be imagined, therefore, a changeless thing of beauty, purged of shapelessness and commonness induced by labour, himself a self-begotten and self-delighting marble or bronze. "It is even possible that being is only possessed completely by the dead"; we return to the ambiguous life or death of the Image. Those who generate and die, perpetually imperfect in their world of becoming, have praise only for that

world; the old man has no part in it, praising only the withered tree and the dry well, hoping only for escape into the world
of complete being, the world of the self-begotten. "The artifice
of eternity", like "the body of this death", is a reversible
term.

'Sailing to Byzantium' could scarcely be regarded as less
than a profoundly considered poem; yet Yeats was willing to
accept the criticism of the acute Sturge Moore that the antithesis of the birds of the dying generations and the golden
bird was imperfect; and this consideration was one of the
causes of the second poem, 'Byzantium'. "Your *Sailing to
Byzantium*," wrote Moore, "magnificent as the first three stanzas
are, lets me down in the fourth, as such a goldsmith's bird is as
much nature as man's body, especially if it only sings like
Homer and Shakespeare of what is past or passing or to come
to Lords and Ladies." Yeats sent him a copy of 'Byzantium' so
that he should have an idea of what was needed for the symbolic cover design of his new book (at this time he was going
to call it not *The Winding Stair* but *Byzantium*) and added that
Moore's criticism was the origin of the new poem — it had
shown the poet that "the idea needed exposition". Only a little
earlier, by the way, Moore had provided Yeats with a copy of
Flecker's 'A Queen's Song', which has a certain relevance to
'Byzantium', being a treatment of the topic of living beauty
versus bronze and marble, or in this instance, gold:

> Had I the power
> To Midas given of old
> To touch a flower
> And leave its petal gold
> I then might touch thy face,
> Delightful boy,
> And leave a metal grace
> A graven joy.
>
> Thus would I slay –
> Ah! desperate device! –
> The vital day
> That trembles in thine eyes,
> And let the red lips close
> Which sang so well
> And drive away the rose
> To leave a shell.

We have already seen why Yeats was so interested in Byzantine art; it gave him that sense of an image totally estranged from specifically human considerations (and particularly from discursive intellect) with meaning and form identical, the vessel of the spectator's passion, which led him to develop the Dancer image. These lines of Flecker point also towards that life-in-death, death-in-life, which characterises the perfect being of art. The absolute difference, as of different orders of reality, between the Image and what is, in the usual sense, alive, was the crucial point upon which the first Byzantium poem had, on Moore's view, failed; it was so important to the poet that he did his work again, making the distinction more absolute, seeking some more perfect image to convey the quality, out of nature and life and becoming, of the apotheosized marble and bronze. The bird must absolutely be a bird of artifice; the entire force of the poem for Yeats depended upon this — otherwise he would scarcely have bothered about Moore's characteristic, and of course intelligent, quibble. Professor N. Jeffares has shown how full are the opening lines of 'Sailing to Byzantium' of peculiarly powerful suggestions of natural life, the life of generation; the salmon carries obvious suggestions of sexual vigour, and, it might be added, of that achieved physical beauty Yeats so much admired, immense power and utter singleness of purpose, in the business of generating and dying. Of course the golden bird must be the antithesis of this, as well as the heavenly counterpart of old scarecrows. It prophesies, speaks out as the foolish and passionate need not; it uses the language of courtesy in a world where all the nature-enforced discriminations of spirit and body, life and death, being and becoming, are meaningless. "Marbles of the dancing floor / Break bitter furies of complexity". And it is this world that Byzantium symbolises. Mr. Jeffares says the bird is different in the second poem because "here it is explicitly contrasted with natural birds, to their disadvantage". In fact the same contrast is intended in the earlier poem; the new degree of explicitness is what Moore's criticism forced upon the poet. The focus of attention is no longer on the poignancy of the contrast between nature and art in these special senses; nature now becomes "mere complexities, The fury and the mire," and the strategy of the poem is, clearly, to establish the immense paradoxical vitality of the dead, more alive than the living; still, but richer in movement than the endless agitation of becoming.

And this is precisely the concept of the dead face and the dancer, the mind moving like a top, which I am calling the central icon of Yeats and of the whole tradition. Byzantium is where this is the normal condition, where all is image and there are no contrasts and no costs, inevitable concomitants of the apparition of absolute being in the sphere of becoming. We can harm the poem by too exclusive an attention to its eschatology, and it is salutary to read it simply as a marvellously contrived emblem of what Yeats took the work of art to be. There is no essential contradiction between the readings. The reconciling force is Imagination, the creator of the symbol by which men "dream and so create Translunar paradise". Or, to use the completely appropriate language of Blake, "This world of Imagination is the world of Eternity; it is the divine bosom into which we shall all go after the death of the Vegetated body. This World of Imagination is Infinite & Eternal, whereas the world of Generation, or Vegetation, is Finite & Temporal.. The Human Imagination. . . appear'd to Me. . . throwing off the Temporal that the Eternal might be Establish'd. . . In Eternity one Thing never Changes into another Thing. Each Identity is Eternal". There is no better gloss on Yeats's poem, a poem impossible outside the tradition of the Romantic Image and its corollary, the doctrine of necessary isolation and suffering in the artist.

In poems later than these, Yeats continues the search for the reconciling image; and he constantly recurs to the theme of remorse, the lost perfection of the life. His 'Dejection Ode', at last, is 'The Circus Animal's Desertion'. The poet sought a theme, without finding one:

> Maybe at last, being but a broken man,
> I must be satisfied with my heart. . .

The 'heart' is the self, speaking out stilled fury and lifeless mire; it is that which has been denied for the work. He enumerates the old themes which had served in the past to cheat the heart, and presents them all, unfairly bitter, as the consolations merely of his own imperfection and estrangement. Oisin was sent through the islands of "vain gaiety, vain battle, vain repose" to satisfy an amorous need in the poet; *The*

Countess Cathleen had its origin in a private fear for a mistress, but "soon enough

> This dream itself had all my thought and love.

And this was the way with all his themes.

> And when the Fool and Blind Man stole the bread
> Cuchulain fought the ungovernable sea;
> Heart-mysteries there, and yet when all is said
> It was the dream itself enchanted me:
> Character isolated by a deed
> To engross the present and dominate memory.
> Players and painted stage took all my love,
> And not those things that they were emblems of.

"Players and painted stage" are here the dream, the work of imagination which relegates 'real' life to a position of minor importance. Hence the final stanza; like the fresh images of Byzantium, these images begin in fury and mire, among the dying generations, and are changed in the dream of imagination. When this no longer works, the poet falls back into the "formless spawning fury", left to live merely, when living is most difficult, life having been used up in another cause.

> Those masterful images because complete
> Grew in pure mind, but out of what began?
> A mound of refuse or the sweepings of a street,
> Old kettles, old bottles, and a broken can,
> Old iron, old bones, old rags, that raving slut
> That keeps the till. Now that my ladder's gone,
> I must lie down where all the ladders start,
> In the foul rag-and-bone shop of the heart.

The increasingly autobiographical quality of the later poems is justified precisely by this need to examine the relation of process to product, of dying generations to bronze and marble. We are reminded of the extraordinary proportion of biographical matter in Coleridge's poem, particularly in the first version of it. If we wanted to study Yeats as hero, we could dwell upon the astonishing pertinacity with which he faced, and the integrity with which he solved, a problem which can never be far from the surface of poetry in this tradition; the Image is always likely to be withdrawn, indeed almost any normal biographical situation is likely to cause its withdrawal — this is part of its cost. Coleridge was finished as a poet in his early thirties; Arnold's situation is in this respect rather similar. Yeats often faced the crisis; the *Autobiographies* show how often, and how desperately, and many poems are made out of it. When poetry is Image, life must, as Yeats said, be tragic.

The dead face which has another kind of life, distinct from that human life associated with intellectual activity; the dancer, inseparable from her dance, devoid of expression — that human activity which interferes with the Image — turning, with a movement beyond that of life, in her narrow luminous circle and costing everything; the bronze and marble that does not provide the satisfactions of the living beauty but represent a higher order of truth, of being as against becoming, which is dead only in that it cannot change: these are the images of the Image that I have considered in this Chapter. They culminate, in Yeats, in the Dancer-image of 'Among Schoolchildren'; and so does the image of the Tree. This image summarises the traditional Romantic critical analogy of art as organism, and, while it is intimately related to the doctrine of the Image, as I have described it, one must discuss it in its own context. In a sense the next Chapter will take us no further, except in so far as it clinches my reading of Yeats's 'Among Schoolchildren'; but its relation to the cult of the Image is so close that it has at any rate to be mentioned, and it can be regarded as an excursus, or an attempt to consolidate.

V

THE TREE

<hr>

Art is the Tree of Life. God is Jesus. Science is the
Tree of Death.

BLAKE

We murder to dissect.

WORDSWORTH

THE work of art considered as having "a life of its own",
supplying its own energy, and possessing no detachable
meanings — yielding to no analysis, containing within
itself all that is relevant to itself — the work of art so described
invites an analogy with unconscious organic life, and resists,
not only attempts to discuss it in terms of the intention of the
artist or detachable 'morals' or 'prose contents', but attempts
to behave towards it as if it were a kind of machine. The Image,
indeed, belongs to no natural order of things. It is out of organic life; but it is easier and less dangerous to talk about it in
terms of the organic than in terms of the mechanical. Confusion sometimes results, as in the writings of T. E. Hulme. But
philosophical exactitude is not what we are looking for. The
Image is "dead, yet flesh and bone"; un-vital, yet describable,
almost necessarily, in terms of vitality. Whether the objects of
one's hatred are Bacon, Locke and Newton, or Darwin, Huxley and Lepage, or other monsters chosen by nineteenth-century Frenchmen, one is going, whenever one uses language
about art, to be involved in some organicist challenge to the
basic eighteenth-century mechanistic treatment of the subject.
The most famous statement of this challenge in English is in

Biographia Literaria, where Coleridge refutes Hartley's mechanistic psychology ("objects *as* objects, are essentially fixed and dead," but the product of the imagination is "essentially *vital*" etc.). Before this there had been a prolonged effort by eighteenth-century aestheticians and psychologists in the tradition of Hartley (notably Hazlitt's favourite Tucker and, to a lesser extent Alison, to whom Wordsworth listened) to develop within the Locke-Hartley tradition a certain freedom from pure determinism, without abandoning that uniformity of impulse which made the imagination as much as the memory dependent upon the nervous reorganization of sense-impressions. But however ingenious such attempts might be, they could never have led to an organicist theory of art, because they could only conceive of extremely complicated *mechanical* processes performed upon material supplied by the 'vegetative' world; before anything like the modern aesthetic was possible there had to be a creative imagination, whether in Blake's or Coleridge's sense. When this was achieved it was possible to revive the notion of the work of art as having a life of its own, which it is murder to dissect: a different kind of life from the prose of proposition and explication, whose function is mechanical. For Coleridge a pssage like the one in 'Guilt and Sorrow' that started him on his quest is utterly transformed by the action of imagination, and becomes completely unparaphrasable, a thing with a life of its own, with all its parts in some organic relation; to destroy that relation would be to destroy the poem. The imagination produces a "translucency of the intelligible in the real" (a formula against which T. E. Hulme was always protesting, though at the same time trying to find another way of saying the same thing) and the resultant image is not susceptible to ordinary intellectual analysis, any more than you can describe a tree by cutting it up. Coleridge's terminology for the imagination — as Mr. M. H. Abrams, who has made a thorough study of it, points out — is biological in flavour. The imagination "assimilates", it is the "coadunating faculty" — this term refers to what is now called symbiosis. It "generates and produces a form of its own". "It is astonishing," says Mr. Abrams, "how much of Coleridge's critical writing is couched in terms that are metaphorical for art and literal for a plant: if Plato's dialectic is a wilderness of mirrors, Coleridge's is a very jungle of vegetation." Consider, as particularly apposite to the present argument, a passage on the symbol in *The Statesman's Manual:*

> I seem to behold in the quiet objects on which I am gazing, more than an arbitrary illustration, more than a mere simile, the work of my own fancy. I feel an awe, as if there were before my eyes the same power as that of the reason — the same power in a lower dignity, and therefore a symbol established in the truth of things. I feel it alike, whether I contemplate a single tree or flower, or meditate on vegetation throughout the world, as one of the great organs of the life of nature. Lo! — with the rising sun it commences its outward life and enters into open communion with all the elements at once assimilating them to itself and to each other. At the same moment it strikes its roots and unfolds its leaves, absorbs and respires, steams forth its cooling vapour and finer fragrance, and breathes a repairing spirit, at once the food and tone of the atmosphere, into the atmosphere that feeds *it*. Lo! — at the touch of light how it returns an air akin to light, and yet with the same pulse effectuates its own secret growth, still contracting to fix what expanding it had refined. Lo! — how upholding the ceaseless plastic motion of the parts in the profoundest rest of the whole, it becomes the visible *organismus* of the whole silent or elementary life of nature, and therefore, in incorporating the one extreme becomes the symbol of the other; the natural symbol of that higher life of reason.

'Reason' here means the operation of the whole mind, of which, for Coleridge, the discursive intellect was only a part, though he did not, like Blake and some later writers, outlaw it completely.

Coleridge is talking about life; the mechanistic universe was the universe of death, and so the product of imagination must, antithetically, be vital. This 'vitalism' stems in part from Boehme, whose influence also intervened in the creation of counter-mechanistic aesthetics in Germany and France; but it also takes much from the Germans of Coleridge's own time. The instance that comes first to mind is the famous page in *Wilhelm Meister*, where *Hamlet* is compared to a tree — "it is a trunk with boughs, leaves, buds, blossoms and fruit. Are they not all one, and there by means of each other?" — and this is already a developed critical use of the analogy between the tree and the work of art. It is impermissible to remove even faults, for fear, so to say, of ringing the tree. The analogy is more highly developed in Herder, from whose 'On the Knowing and Feeling of the Human Soul' (1778) Mr. Abrams dates what he calls "the age of biologism", where biology replaces physics as the seminal science, "the great source of concepts which, migrating into other provinces, were modifying the general character of ideation". Herder applies the idea critically to *King Lear*, which he finds to be like the universe in that it is filled with "one interpenetrating, all-animating soul". Incidentally, when such ideas are applied to history, say the history of architecture, we get such equations as Gothic= organic, neo-classic=mechanical, and with the usual load of qualifications imposed by the caution of modern historical scholarship, these analogies are still employed.

It is not my design (nor do I have the knowledge) to trace the history of this analogy from the late eighteenth century to modern criticism, but it is evidently important in the Romantic theory of the Image, and continues to contribute to such modern attitudes as the mistrust of paraphrase, and 'anti-intentionalism'. Even the author has no business to interfere with or explain his work. If it were merely mechanical he could take it back to the drawing-board; but as it is organic, he can only talk about it as everybody else can. Such notions have been commonplace since Coleridge. Carlyle (who of course knew the Goethe passage) uses the tree-image in 'The Hero as Poet', and talks of the poem as having its origin unconsciously in the depths of the poet's being, not in his intellect. Carlyle had some celebrity among the French Symbolists, and this is, of course, a step forward from Coleridge, though Carlyle is not talking about the modern unconscious; there is no hint of surrealism, and for him such a poem is a moral act nonetheless. Already in the mid-nineteenth century it was common ground that the image, rather than the mechanics of discourse, was the true mark of poetry. It was called 'the sensuous concrete' by one critic; another argued that the imagination presents "concretions of diverse phenomena organized into phenomenal unity by the pervading vital influence of a subjective idea"; another that the words must be "alive with presentative significance", must present "real, living objects" (See A. H. Warren,

English Poetic Theory, 1825-1865). And all this in an age when, according to a doctrine still current, poets were thinking and feeling separately, not 'thinking in images', but uneasily discoursing. Certainly to think in images was the advice of many critics from Coleridge to Arthur Hallam and beyond. Now the point about such images — the images available to so special a sensibility — is that they are body-and-soul together, meaning what they are, possessing organic vitality because they behave like the tree and the dancer. Discourse, thinking in concepts, is, in contrast, mechanical.

Even Arnold, notorious for his insistence on the mechanical aspects of architectonic — more akin, in Coleridge's terminology, to 'shape' than to 'form' — and his disturbance at the bad habit of poets who concentrated on the detail rather than the design, was well aware of this organic-mechanistic antithesis. He was of course steeped in Burke, and seems to have known Coleridge's distinction between 'culture' and 'civilisation'; and in poetry he did not want to "solve the universe" but to "reconstruct" it (by which he must mean something like Herder's claim for *King Lear*) and to get, like Shakespeare, "the movement and fulness of life itself." The work must be filled with "one interpenetrating, all-animating soul". It must have a life of its own, its life and its beauty being the same thing. It must be like a tree.

I do not suggest that Yeats himself had the historical background of the tree image in mind when he used it; and in any case the direct line of descent in his case runs not from the Germans and Coleridge but from Blake, who makes a very large contribution to Yeats's aesthetic. One may see something of this, without leaving the tree-image, by a glance at Yeats's poem 'The Two Trees', published in *The Rose* (1893). This poem is obviously based on a lyric in Blake's *Poetical Sketches* —

> Love and harmony combine,
> And around our souls entwine,
> While thy branches mix with mine,
> And our roots together join.
>
> Joys upon our branches sit,
> Chirping loud, and singing sweet;
> Like gentle streams beneath our feet
> Innocence and virtue meet.

Thou the golden fruit dost bear,
I am clad in flowers fair;
Thy sweet boughs perfume the air,
And the turtle buildeth there.

There she sits and feeds her young,
Sweet I hear her mournful song;
And thy lovely leaves among,
There is love; I hear his tongue.

There his charming nest doth lay,
There he sleeps the night away;
There he sports along the day,
And doth among our branches play.

This is a poem of innocence; of innocent sexuality, in fact. The tree has in it no positive trace of the enormous symbolism it was later to carry in Blake, best summed up perhaps in the brief antithesis "Art is the Tree of Life... Science is the Tree of Death" (*The Laocoon Group*) but it is clearly the Tree of Life. Yeats was of course interested from the start in the mature symbolism of the two Trees, for the first symbolised the creative and redemptive imagination and the second all barrenly discursive and prudential knowledge; "men who sought their food among the green leaves of the Tree of Life condemned none but the unimaginative and the idle, and those who forget that even love and death and old age are an imaginative art," as Yeats explains it in *Ideas of Good and Evil*. The good tree is desire and divine energy, the bad is morality and nature, the fallen world, selfhood and abstraction. All this symbolism Yeats is trying to incorporate in what appears an insubstantial song. He used it again in an interesting prose passage called 'The Tree of Life' which is closely associated with 'The Guitar Player', and which makes much of Verlaine and the argument that "We artists have taken over much to heart that old commandment about seeking after the Kingdom of Heaven". It is a very Blakean remark; and Yeats could always see French Symbolism in Blakean terms. His poem even imitates the movement of Blake's, but he introduces a schematic contrast between the Tree of life and the Tree of knowledge or death, which derives from the more developed symbolism of his author. Here, in very early Yeats, we have a theme closely

related to that of the dancer expressed in terms of the organicist tree-analogu, yet almost completely derived from Blake.

> Beloved, gaze in thine own heart,
> The holy tree is growing there;
> From joy the holy branches start,
> And all the trembling flowers they bear.
> The changing colours of its fruit
> Have dowered the stars with merry light;
> The surety of its hidden root
> Has planted quiet in the night;
> The shaking of its leafy head
> Has given the waves their melody.
> And made my lips and music wed,
> Murmuring a wizard song for thee.
> There, through bewildered branches, go
> Winged Loves borne on in gentle strife,
> Tossing and tossing to and fro
> The flaming circle of our life.
> When looking on their shaken hair,
> And dreaming how they dance and dart,
> Thine eyes grow full of tender care;
> Beloved, gaze in thine own heart.

Here, well concealed in the Blakean simplicities that are
mostly direct borrowings, are the properties of the Tree of
Imagination. The branches are 'holy'; they start from 'joy'.
The tree is responsible for a universal harmony, the prereq-
uisite of traditional symbolist systems, and also for the song
of poets. It is inhabited by Love, and it grows in the heart of a
woman who is beautiful and does not think. If she does so she
is gazing at another Tree:

> Gaze no more in the bitter glass
> The demons, with their subtle guile,
> Lift up before us when they pass,
> Or only gaze a little while;
> For there a fatal image grows,
> With broken boughs and blackened leaves,
> And roots half hidden under snows
> Driven by a storm that ever grieves.
> For all things turn to barrenness
> In the dim glass the demons hold,

> The glass of outer weariness,
> Made when God slept in times of old.
> There, though the broken branches, go
> The ravens of unresting thought;
> Peering and flying to and fro,
> To see men's souls bartered and bought.
> When they are heard upon the wind,
> And when they shake their wings, alas!
> Thy tender eyes grow all unkind;
> Gaze no more in the bitter glass.

It is needless to say how close this is to the theme of woman's beauty bartered for argument, the brawling of the market-place bringing a shrill voice and hard eyes; beauty, whether of the body or of art, is broken by an act of homage to the abstract, as Eve bowed to the tree when she had eaten the apple. This second tree, for Yeats and Blake, is the tree of the Fall. The other is the tree of Life, the vitality of the body of the Image. It has some part in the figure of the green laurel so beautifully used in 'A Prayer for My Daughter'; and after many years, when Yeats came to revise this little early poem, he made changes only to achieve more violent emphases in his later manner:

> There the Loves a circle go,
> The flaming circle of our days,
> Gyring, spiring to and fro
> In those great ignorant leafy ways –

it is not the gyres that are important here, but the emphatic 'ignorant' — this is the anti-intellectualist tree.

> . . .Flying, crying, to and fro,
> Cruel claw and hungry throat,
> Or else they stand and sniff the wind,
> And shake their ragged wings. . .

The vulture image enhances the dead rottenness of the second tree; it is one of the poems Yeats improved by revision, and the reason is probably that he had never ceased to live with its images, so early taken from Blake to become part of his own mind.

For it is a fact that nearly all Yeats's later thought develops from a position — or is intruded into a pattern — already formed when he made his edition of Blake. In the field of aesthetics this first tree is the quasi-instinctive, happy, self-begotten work of imaginative art; the second is that of the reason which, as a merely reflective faculty, partakes of death (for in this loose philosophical context the words of Blake and Coleridge are often interchangeable). In many other related ways also the relation with Blake persists. There is the fundamental insistence upon the inseparability of soul and body — "the notion that a man has a body distinct from his soul must be expunged" — which is reflected in Yeats's theory of education as well as in his Symbolist theory of the Image; neither the beautiful woman nor the Image she emblematizes must be surrendered to the Spectre. Similar opinions are common in Symbolist aesthetics, and were influentially stated by Gourmont (see Pound's essay on this author); but Yeats, like Symons, had already been prepared for the French theories by Blake and Pater. Similarly the practical requirements of the Symbolist artist (concreteness and the scrupulous exclusion of *insignificant* detail from the organic design) were perfectly familiar to students of Blake and his disciples, all, as Yeats said, Symbolists *avant la lettre*. Blake's conviction of the paramount importance of distinctness in perception and so in the artist's outline — and of what were for the hated Locke secondary qualities, like redness in roses, hardness in diamonds — and of what he called 'minute particulars' — are echoed in Yeats. The love of clear outline, the first requirement of *Dinglichkeit*, has indeed important implications for image-theory in Blakean thinkers. "All depends on Form and Outline"; Blake constantly insists upon the need for concreteness, preferring the sharp outline of the childish perception to that control of the abstract and general that comes with maturity. But this concreteness and definition is not in nature, which for Blake is fallen; it is the gift of divine imagination. The artist *makes* the eternal world; it is the product of his Imagination. The great tree itself, the organicist image, is not, in Blakean terms, a vegetable tree; if it were it would be dead. Only the imagination can make it live as a symbol, and that is the true life. Pursuing this notion in less exalted terms, Blake anticipates much modern aesthetic with his argument that conception and execution are, in the artist, the same act. "I have heard many People say, 'Give me the Ideas. It is no matter what Words you put them into,' & others say, 'Give me the Design, it is no matter for the Execution.' These People know Enough of Artifice, but Nothing of Art. Ideas cannot be Given but in their minutely Appropriate Words, nor Can a Design be made without its minutely Appropriate Execution. . . He who copies does not Execute; he only Imitates what is already Executed. Execution is only the result of Invention." The most notable modern defence of this position is Collingwood's. But here it is soberly expressed; and for Blake, and after him Yeats, it is more usual to think of the Imagination as divine, and as conferring symbolic concreteness, by means of what we call art, on the fallen world; "Nature has no outline, but Imagination has. . . Nature has no Supernatural and dissolves: Imagination is Eternity". The act of conception-execution is a symbol-making act; it confers significance, makes a live thing of which the mode of existence is not temporal at all, and which is variously represented, under different aspects, by such images as those of the Dancer and the Tree.

The artist who performs this act is a man inspired and apart; but he has no rights over the Image. Blake is completely 'anti-intentionalist'; witness his remark on Wordsworth's Preface. The Wordsworth who matters was the maker of symbols — the Leech Gatherer, the tree "of many one"; these place him among the great artists ("but there is no competition"). The other, mechanistic, Wordsworth, was the sane reasonable man who failed to see that natural objects deaden and was constantly abstracting from his vision, having misunderstood his own poetry. Here are two more beliefs Yeats shared: he distrusted explanations, even his own, and he distrusted Imitation, because it is always abstraction. It is not the poet's business to reproduce the appearances of the fallen world and make abstractions from it; the sons of Albion did that when they made "an Abstract, which is a negation Not only of the Substance from which it is derived. . . but also a murderer Of every Divine member". Yeats always professed his hatred of abstraction, his adherence to the Blakean doctrine of concretion, firmness of outline; and frequently, in those excellent essays on Blake, asserted the master's teaching on Imitation. He quotes with particular approval the requirement of "distinct, sharp and wiry" bounding lines, though with the qualification that Blake, in his "visionary realism", forgot how colour and shadow may assist this prime requirement, and "compel the canvas or paper to become itself a symbol of some not indefinite because unsearchable essence" — words which link Blake with the ultimate definitions of the Symbol in Yeats's own time. Above all, Yeats was in complete sympathy with Blake's plea for the formal significance of every part of a painting or poem. That is why he studied Palmer and Calvert, and why the 'touchstones' of poetic symbolism provided in the essay called 'The Symbolism of Poetry' are all verses which derive their power from internal reference: their quality, that is, is dependent upon the organisms to which they belong, like the dancer upon the dance, and the blossom upon the tree. That is what distinguishes this true Symbolist writing from the wrong kind of poetry, the kind that was, he hoped, being superseded: "descriptions of nature for the sake of nature, of the moral law for the sake of the moral law. . . brooding over scientific opinion", poetry in which sense and spirit, body and soul, were dissociated.

The Tree is in a sense necessary to the Dancer, since it so powerfully reinforces the idea of integrity — "root, shoot, blossom" — in the Image, and provides a traditional analogy in support of the Image's independent life. It is fitting that the two emblems should have been fused in 'Among Schoolchildren', where the cost in life to the artist is also so wonderfully involved. The poem is the fullest expression of Yeats's mature attitude to the whole question of art in life, and it is characteristic that its elements had been in his mind for many years, conducing to what he would have called tragedy in his life, but also towards this, the greatest of his victories over 'outward fate'.

The Tree in Yeats is not a merely personal symbol. He learnt it in the first place from Blake, who more than any other artist formed his mind; and it is therefore profoundly associated with the tradition in which he wrote, and with the attempt to restore to art that integrity which it could possess only if it were to become once again truly Symbolist; which is to say, recover those images of truth which have nothing to do with the intellect of scientists, nothing to do with time. They exist beyond the possibility of dissociation (even in the paraphrase of critics) in a condition of perfect unity and vitality ('integrity, consonance and clarity' said Stephen Dedalus).

And, though few have written about it so fully and frankly as Yeats, this is the effort of all the major poets in the Romantic tradition — and the critics too. We shall see, in the second part of this essay, some of the curious disguises under which the Image, and also the concept of the isolated artist, appear in the main tradition of modern writing.

PART TWO

THE TWENTIETH CENTURY

───────

My true life is in the unspoken words of my body.

Ezra Pound, after Remy de Gourmont

VI

ARTHUR SYMONS

For things below are copies, the Great Smaragd-
ine Tablet said...

YEATS

WHEN we come to consider how the twentieth century
has used these ideas, we are obliged, I think, to regard
Arthur Symons as crucial. He, more explicitly and
more influentially than any of his contemporaries, saw how to
synthesise the earlier English tradition — particularly Blake,
on whom he wrote a good, and in this connexion revealing,
book — with Pater and those European Symbolists he knew so
well. Symons also had a considerable part in the associated
revival of interest in Donne and the Jacobean dramatic poets.
But above all he wrote the book out of which the important
poets of the early twentieth century learnt the elements of
French Symbolist poetic.

It is not really surprising that what is often regarded as
Symbolist influence in Yeats can be traced to earlier English
Romantic thought, and specifically to Blake. 'Movements' are
never as new as they look: it is one of the duller laws of literary
history. And the similarities between the French doctrines and
those of Blake were early recognized; Blake was welcomed, by
others before Yeats himself, as a forerunner of Symbolism.
Nearly all the Symbolists supposed that they were finding again
something that had been lost, or that they were merely the

107

first people to be fully conscious of something that was in fact necessary to all great art. Blake was the 'chanticleer' of their new dawn, proclaiming unambiguously what was to them of high importance: "The world of imagination is infinite and eternal". A poet with his head full of Blake would see without surprise certain similarities between his own way of thinking and that of the new writers in France. It has even been suggested that Yeats knew these poets only at second hand, although he met and admired Verlaine.

There is an amusing contrast between Yeats's portrait of Verlaine and that of the man who best understood these relationships, and to whom Yeats owed much of his knowledge of French aesthetic, Arthur Symons. Yeats's is full of his curious humour, a humour based on a cautiously critical attitude to human beings, unabated by his intense admiration for all Verlaine represented. Symons, on the other hand, chants a solemn hymn of praise, entirely without mitigating comment, of both man and poet (for Verlaine was honoured by the English disciples as the greatest of the movement). This totally uncritical attitude in Symons implies, perhaps, the lack of a quality desirable in a man undertaking the task he chose, but for all that English poetry and criticism have been changed by his book *The Symbolist Movement in Literature* (1899), and that is as much as a critic can achieve. As I have said, it was the first book of its kind, and the work from which other important poets besides Yeats learnt the elements of the subject; and it was certainly none the worse for Symons's knowledge of Blake. That *The Symbolist Movement* is absolutely a good book I suppose nobody would suggest. It is scrappy, lacking the pertinacity we have come to expect from critics; it is often disagreeably imprecise. As a simple exposition of its subject it has of course been superseded. But it is a very good place to look if one wants to know how French Symbolism struck a well-informed, avant-garde Paterian in the 'nineties; and considering that the character of modern poetry has been, to a remarkable degree, formed by that contact, we may well think it worth while to do so.

Symons's book is dedicated to Yeats, and his prefatory letter, insisting upon the European diffusion of the new movement, calls Yeats "the chief representative of that movement in our country". It also refers to the author's own growing interest in what he calls Mysticism, which he evidently regards as a related subject, and of which he treats Yeats as a master. This is an interesting connexion, and I shall return to it. Of course Symons had much better have said Magic, and the allusion is to Yeats's interest in occult theologies of the hermetic and cabbalistic tradition. 'Tradition' is the right word, for there are recognisable affinities between Hermes Trismegistus, the Neo-Platonists, Agrippa, Boehme, Swedenborg and Blake on the one hand, and the alchemists and theurgists of the Renaissance, with their curious descendants, on the other. Symons did well to mention the connexion between Magic and Symbolism early. It is an important one, by no means as isolated from the concerns of modern poetry as might appear; this will emerge as we consider his book.

It begins with a short and inadequate introductory chapter of a theoretical nature, which is probably most interesting when related to Symons's own poetry. Then a chapter apiece is devoted to the more important Symbolists from de Nerval to Huysmans and Maeterlinck. Some of these essays are of small value, but there are scattered observations of interest, and the chapter on Mallarmé is a more serious effort. I shall simply, without trying to summarise, and digressing whenever commentary seems to be needed, indicate what seems to retain importance.

For Symons, the Movement is essentially a revolution against "the contemplation and rearrangement of material things" considered as normal art. He cites Carlyle's definition of the Symbol — a definition which had been widely circulated in France, where Taine had reported the relevant chapter in *Sartor Resartus* — as "an embodiment and revelation of the infinite", "concealment yet revelation". The Decadence he regards simply as an inferior forerunner of Symbolism, calling attention to the predominantly philological metaphor implied by the term: it applies mainly to style, to "that ingenious deformation of language" by which Mallarmé and the rest enter into competition with "the Greek and Latin of the Decadence". (Earlier, in a paper of 1893, he had given a different definition, calling Decadence "oversubtilising refinement upon refinement, a spiritual and moral perversity". "Ces chers poèmes," said Mallarmé of the literature of Rome's last agony, "dont les plaques de fard ont plus de charme sur moi que l'incarnat de la jeunesse.") But in any case Symbolism was much more, nothing less than "an attempt to spiritualise literature, to evade the old bondage of rhetoric, the old bondage of exteriority. . . Description is banished that beautiful things may be evoked, magically". It is by the Symbol that "the soul of things can be made visible".

The main psychological assumption of Symbolism (from which it derives an audience for itself) is essentially that of early Romantic aesthetic: that the human mind is so constituted as to be able to recognize images of which it can have no perceived knowledge — the magic assumption, or the assumption that makes so much of dreams. That the whole work of art should be regarded as such an image would not have surprised Coleridge, nor, for that matter, Blake, though he might have put it very differently. Symons, indeed, saw that, although Blake's "whole mental attitude was opposed to that of the practisers of magic", he had nevertheless the root of this matter in him: "To Blake, to be 'myself alone, shut up in myself' was to be in no merely individual but in a universal world, that world of imagination whose gates seemes to him to be open to every human being". This is what Symons, using his new critical language, was after. But he was emphasising the magical analogy, giving the Symbol the same relation to spiritual reality as the daemonic 'sign' of the mage. It has the same qualities, on his view, of absolute revelation (it is the concrete embodiment of a supernatural entity) and arcane concealment (it is in no sense representational) that the sign has. And misty as all this may sound, I do not think the commonplace modern conception of the work of art as some sort of complex image, autotelic, liberated from discourse, with coincident form and meaning, could have evolved — as it clearly did — from Symbolist aesthetic if there had not been such a *rapprochement* between poet and occultist. Magic came, in an age of science, to the defence of poetry. In fact Symons, on grounds that Arnold might not have fully approved, calls the literature of the movement "a new kind of religion, with all the duties and responsibilities of the sacred ritual". Others spoke of poets as a third order of priesthood.

Some of this Symons got from Yeats, who regarded his magical studies as essential to his poetry — his essay on 'Magic' in *Ideas of Good and Evil*, with its emphasis on the power of the

Image not only to wake analogies but also to penetrate to the Great Memory, has long been regarded as fundamental to his work. But Symons was also indebted directly to his French sources. He shows great interest in Nerval's *Le Rêve et la Vie*, particularly in a passage which deals with the doctrines of synaesthesia and *correspondance* — characteristic Symbolist preoccupations — and comments thus:

> To have realised that central secret of the mystics, from Pythagoras onwards, the secret which the Smaragdine Tablet of Hermes betrays in its "As things are below, so they are above"; which Boehme has classed in his teaching of "signatures" and Swedenborg has systematised in his doctrine of "correspondences"; does it matter very much that he arrived at it by way of the obscure and fatal initiation of madness?

For to Nerval (whose madness is of so little account) this revelation brought the celebrity of having "divined, before all the world, that poetry should be a miracle; not a hymn to beauty, not the description of beauty, nor beauty's mirror; but beauty itself, the colour, fragrance and form of the imagined flower, as it blossoms again out of the page". Here the hermetic tradition and Symbolism become almost indistinguishable; and the truth is that the whole poetic movement was to a striking degree hermetic; the occult tradition, notably as mediated by Boehme and Swedenborg, lies behind it as it lies behind Blake and some seventeenth-century poetry. When Yeats wrote his long commentary on "correspondence" in Blake, for the edition, he made the same distinction between 'perpendicular' and 'longitudinal' correspondences in his author that recent scholars (like M. Georges Blin) have introduced into the study of Baudelaire. The connexions at which I am here hinting were perfectly familiar to Yeats and Symons in the 'nineties, and although they have been partly forgotten, their effects are still to be detected in some of the assumptions of modern poetic, most of all in its persistent attempts to produce the equivalent of the 'metaphysical' conceit, which contemporary criticism justified by arguments drawn from a metaphysic of correspondence.

This metaphysic descended in a tenuous but unbroken line from the Renaissance to the Romantic movement, and emerged in a form significant for poetry as early as Blake and Novalis. In early nineteenth-century France there was considerable interest in the occult, though apparently with little attempt to discriminate between the genuine practitioner and the quack (a recurring feature of the history of magic). Baudelaire must have known about the various kinds of Illuminisme and masonry, and he greatly admired de Maistre; he was also aware of Nerval's curious effort, worthy of the Florentine Platonists, to gather together and use the occult potentialities of all religions. Balzac's story *Séraphitâ*, a work much read by Symbolists, tells of men who understood "the invisible bonds by which the material worlds are attached to the spiritual, and who found "le principe des melodies en entendant les chants du ciel qui donnaient les sensations des couleurs, des parfums, de la pensée". Here is both longitudinal (synaesthetic) and perpendicular (hermetic) correspondence. This aspect of occultism goes hand in hand with the Romantic movement in France, and might have done in England if Blake had had his due. To Yeats and Symons it was clear that the magic element must be re-introduced, in order to affirm, or re-affirm, the status of the Image as a means of tapping "l'inépuisable fonds de l'universelle analogie". The French had made this a central doctrine, after Baudelaire had affirmed that the imagination was the faculty which grasped the analogies and rendered them as symbols. Symbols are, simply, images with this essential magical power.

Now this makes the modern symbol resemble, in some ways, kinds of image used in seventeenth-century poetry. For example, it seems certain that behind the emblems so fashionable in that period — they are best known to us in the pietistic forms which came to exert, through Jesuit propaganda, a direct influence on Baroque art and poetry — was a justification in pure Neo-Platonic terms of the aniconic image presented as the only possible representative of some reality imperceptible to the senses and without phenomenal equivalent. This kind of image, as it appears in poetry, is something quite different from allegory; and the easiest way of distinguishing it is, interestingly enough, in Blake's terms. As Yeats put it,

William Blake was the first writer of modern times to preach the indissoluble marriage of all great art with symbol. There had been allegorists and teachers of allegory in plenty, but the symbolic imagination, or, as Blake preferred to all it, 'vision', is not allegory, being 'a representation of what actually exists really and unchangeably.' A symbol is indeed the only possible expression of some invisible essence, a transparent lamp about a spiritual flame; while allegory is one of many possible representations of an embodied thing or familiar principle, and belongs to fancy, and not to imagination: the one is a revelation, the other an amusement.

The reference is to Blake's *Vision of the Last Judgment*, and a passage of greater import than Yeats suggests, since it expressly excludes allegory as "Form'd by the daughters of Memory" and argues that "Vision or Imagination" is the highest knowledge". "Plato has made Socrates say that Poets & Prophets do not know or Understand what they write or Utter; this is a most Pernicious Falshood. If they do not, pray is an inferior kind to be call'd Knowing?" To this straightforward (and very Symbolist) way of putting it, Yeats has preferred a manner that incorporates the formulae of Coleridge. But the point is that Blake's position on allegory and symbol would have been acceptable to many seventeenth-century poets, who were also perfectly familiar with the doctrine of correspondence used as metaphysical support for image-theory. Their magic (for that is what it amounts to) is virtually the same as that which lay behind the later movement; the theory of correspondences enabled the aestheticians of the nineteenth-century to revive, as if they were new things, doctrines commonplace in 1600. Of course there are accidental differences, and the later poets made a formidable body of German philosophy support the traditional metaphysic, but the similarities are none the less substantial. And this is why I have allowed myself to digress from the consideration of Symons's book: these similarities are important. The development of Symbolist thought in England could not have proceeded far before somebody saw that there was matter for thought in seventeenth-century poetry. Symons did see this, and had a lively interest in Donne and the drama of that period, as any Symbolist historian of literature would. And, as the present century has so strongly associated its poetic with the Donne revival, it seems important, and this seems the place, to sketch very briefly the reason why it ever became possible to think of Laforgue and Donne, Webster and Villiers de l'Isle Adam, as poets of the same sort. Symons, in fact, makes intelligible a habit that came to dominate twentieth-century criticism in its historical phase. I return to this matter in the next chapter but one; let me now get back to Symons's book.

He writes, as I have said, with uncritical adulation of Verlaine, treating him (no wonder it was though dangerous) as the pattern of Pater's perfect man as he deduced him from the original conclusion of *The Renaissance*. It was Verlaine who broke the rhetorical tradition of French poetry, who wrote poems "which go as far as verse can go to become pure music", in whom "the sense of hearing and the sense of sight are almost interchangeable". We may remember that Yeats's view of Verlaine was almost identical with this; personally, as well as in his poetry, the French poet stood for much that Yeats admired. Symons, strangely enough, makes a pair, a sort of Yeatsian antithesis, of Rimbaud and Verlaine, "the man of action" and "the man of sensation", and perhaps it should be attributed to Yeats's patchy reading that he nowhere, so far as I can remember, alludes to Rimbaud, who would have been a wonderful asset to the System.

The essay on Mallarmé is more important. Symons distinguishes three periods in this author: the first of clear and beautiful poems, the last of "opaque darkness", and a middle period, represented by the *Hérodiade* and *L'Après-midi d'un Faune*, which he regards as the summit of the poet's achievement, for "every word is a jewel. . . every image is a symbol, and the whole poem is visible music". What I should like here to direct attention to is what he had to say about the last period. On Symons's view, this is the expression of a devotion to silence, an isolated, solipsist poetry. And I think it is greatly to Symons's credit that he saw in these last works of Mallarmé a certain danger latent in Symbolist poetic. I think he may have communicated this understanding to Yeats, who, from the earliest days right up to the time when he made little jokes about nobody really understanding what he was talking about, was always concerned with the danger of stepping over into un-communication, into an area where the magic bond between poet and audience should be broken. What Mallarmé aspired to, according to Symons, was a liberation of the soul in literature from "the body of that death"; in other words, to the idea of the autonomous Image, free of discursive content. The purpose of all his care was "to evoke, by some elaborate, instantaneous magic of language, without the formality of an after all impossible description", this image - again we hear the inescapable language of magic; but behind Symons's remarks there is an undoubted commonsense.

In effect, he accuses the poet of going too far in his pursuit of the ultimate aim, "to be, rather than to express". He was perfectly aware of the difficulty, which he elsewhere discusses, of working, in an art that aspired to the condition of music, with words that derive their meanings in unmusical ways, and this seemed to him to set limits to the Symbolist aspiration, limits which Mallarmé had transgressed. The language in which he makes his accusation is drawn, whether accidentally or not I cannot say, from the terminology of the old controversy over alchemy. "To say that he had found what he sought is impossible; but (is it possible to avoid saying?) how heroic a search, and what marvellous discoveries on the way!" Mallarmé is the alchemist; he does not find the Stone, but he stumbles, in his search for it, on such fascinating compounds that we are very willing, in Donne's phrase, to glorify his pregnant pot. But the result of his efforts in the later poems, the final stages of the projection, is merely that 'the work', as an alchemist would say, returns to chaos. A poem like *Un Coup de Dès* achieves an obscurity practically impenetrable to any but the poet, and only the discoveries 'on the way' remain; these of course are great discoveries. Symons saw the dangers, but he also saw the whole future of poetry in Mallarmé's achievement: "It is on the lines of that spiritualising of the word, that perfecting of form in its capacity for allusion and suggestion, that confidence in the eternal correspondences between the visible and invisible universe, which Mallarmé taught, and too intermittently practised, that literature must now move, if it is in any sense to move forward."

So Symons, in prophesying the immediate future of poetry, prophesied also its dangers. He was acutely aware of the Symbolist paradox that art is both concrete and obscure. "All art hates the vague," he says in the essay on Maeterlinck; yet the Mallarméan method holds out little hope of avoiding an obscurity, an impermeability to the ordinary senses of the reader, which may well seem indistinguishable from the vague and indeed the obscurantist, so that the artist loses an audience and wins more hatred and suspicion. Symons welcomed the novels of Huysmans, partly because they tended to prove that Symbolism could 'make sense'; he would not have been surprised that the novel has, in some ways, had more success than poetry in post-Symbolist times. The dangers attending poetry he saw clearly. They were not merely technical. The poetry of isolation, defying philosophical and moral assumptions, and breaking the rule that it 'ought' to 'say' something, would alienate the potential audience still further, and be called obscure because of this failure in communication. The doctrine of correspondences does not in itself conduce to clarity, but Symons was not so much afraid of an exquisite Gongorism as of the failure to remember how limited words were for the purpose. He does not say so, but it looks as if he had some feeling that the symbol must deign to be domesticated in a structure with some appearance of logic, that the 'work' should cease before the whole apparatus blows up *in fumo*. It is the Mallarméan fault of pressing on to that semantic explosion, or near it, that is responsible for the fact that 'obscurity' rather than 'concreteness' is the first word that occurs to a literate non-specialist public when it thinks of modern poetry. When poetry is by definition *inexplicable* (Nerval said it of his sonnets, and poets have been saying it ever since) only an act of magic can effect communication (as M. Béguin says of his Romantic poet, "s'il est un vrai magicien. . . le miracle se produira"). But there was, as Symons feared, a point beyond which irrational disorder ought not to go, if the miracle was to have any chance of happening.

It is hardly too much to say that the Symbolist movement was not only the cause of many of the varieties of modern obscurity, but also of the critical techniques that have been evolved in order that such poetry may be inoffensively discussed; and of course these techniques have been applied to other poetry on the assumption that it is basically (if it is any good) Symbolist in character — a view shared, though very differently implemented, by critics as far apart as Symons and Mr. Cleanth Brooks. It is surely significant that so many of the recurring problems of the modern critic are related to those arising in Symbolist aesthetic; examples are the problem of poetry and belief, and that of the possibility of long poems. The first is a variant of the question about the discursive element in art. The second, usually derived direct from Poe, is extremely common. Symons already shows a troubled awareness of it, and it is, of course basic in a poetic which rejects nearly all the conditions by which the long poem exists. Rather than retail a list of distinguished critics who testify to the impossibility of the long poem, I will borrow a parable.

Happening upon Alfred Poizat's book *Le Symbolisme de Baudelaire à Claudel* (1924), I find him saying that the value of the conversation there reported evaporated when Mallarmé wrote it down.

> Il y a là, évidemment, des choses de toute beauté, pour qui sait les lire, mais c'est très loin de ce que nous avons entendu. Lorsque cet homme parlait, son style atteignait la limite de la perfection; lorsqu'il écrivait, il la dépassait. Sa pensée jaillissait de son âme à ses lèvres, toute formée, toute splendide, définitive, mais, devant le papier blanc, qui, de son propre aveu, lui donna toujours de l'angoisse, elle ne sortait plus que goutte à goutte. Un autre travail intervenait où son souci maladif du fini et du rare le faisait s'acharner au détail, inventer à la phrase de subtiles et neuves articulations, mille jeux savants, des raccourcis incroyables, des malices derrière chaque mot, d'ingénieuses soudures, tout un labyrinthe, ou la pensée s'égare et ne retrouve plus d'issue. Evidemment, quand c'est réussi, c'est extrêmement joli, amusant et même profond, mais cela change la perspective de la pensée et même cela la dénature. C'est de l'art chinois ou japonais.
>
> Il y a, dans toute œuvre d'art, un point de perfection, qu'il ne faut pas dépasser, sous peine de la détruire... Balzac, dans *le Chef-d'oeuvre inconnu*, a déviné et décrit cette maladie du style, qui arrive a détruire une oeuvre, primitivement belle.

The story of Mallarmé destroying his *obiter dicta* is the story of many Symbolist poems. Yet the date of Balzac's story (to which I shall return) was 1832; the warning was sounded early, by a writer the Symbolists respected, and it had not lost its force a century later when Yeats, on two occasions, neatly

117

applied it to Pound's *Cantos*. For the ideograms of that poem are symbols (or Images, or Vortices) which seemed, because of their developed function in Chinese thought, to have some hope of holding together in a structure owing nothing to logic and connective discourse. In this way, and with the aid of music (a fugue has structure but no discursive meaning) a long poem might be possible, whereas if it has to resort to continuous narrative or doctrine it becomes at best a series of short poems tediously bound together by prose. But the difficulties are enormous, in terms of precision and complexity of the symbolic relationships; and the finished product, eschewing all devices which we habitually recognise as establishing connexions, may be nothing but a confused heap of words, with only the isolated perfect detail to show dreadfully the artist has squandered his power. And this is the point of the parable. Before Mallarmé wrote it down, what he said was delightful; and there was delight at some stage of the prehistory of the *Cantos*. But then came the great effort at the purgation of discourse; and such a purgation can only, in a long poem, produce a disaster like that of Balzac's painter.

One might, if one were arguing for an upward estimate of Arthur Symons, contend that he foresaw the probable nature of the problems that would face poets like Pound. Certainly these problems are inherent in the nineteenth-century revaluation of the power and function of the Image, and we must now go on to consider some of the later developments in that effort of revaluation, between Symons and our own time.

VII

T. E. HULME

Literature as entirely the deliberate standing still,
hovering and thinking oneself into an artificial
view, for the moment, and not effecting any real
action at all.

'Notes on Language and Style'

HENCEFORTH we shall be occupied with developments
of the theory of the Image or Symbol which do not
always acknowledge their inheritance, and indeed are
frequently associated with critical positions avowedly hostile
to Romantic aesthetics. More specifically, our concern will be
with the problems of the inheritance for poets and critics who
have difficulty in accepting, in any simple form, the idea of
the magical properties of the Image, or any exact parallel
between poetic and mystical cognition, but who nevertheless
want the work of art quite free of discursive content (itself a
Symbol, or, as Professor Lehmann calls it, an "aesthetic
monad"); and who continue to be motivated, like their predecessors, by a recognition of their duty to distinguish between
art on the one hand, and the positivism or propaganda of most
other activities of the human mind, on the other.

The extraordinary subtleties of argument necessitated by
this situation are naturally not to be found in Symons, yet it is
not easy to overstate his importance as a publicist. Eliot has
said that, but for Symons, he would not, at the critical moment
of his career, have known of Laforgue, admitting that *The
Symbolist Movement* was to this extent formative. Pound, in a

letter to René Taupin of 1928, says that the French influence on him ("Baudelaire, Verlaine, etc.") came *via* Symons, though he adds that, unlike some other members of the *cénacle*, he read the French poets with care and critical severity. Imagism, he says, "doit 'quelquechose' aux symbolistes français via T. E. Hulme, via Yeats < Symons < Mallarmé. Comme le pain doit quelquechose au vanneur de blé, etc."

I do not intend to say anything here about the poetry of Imagism proper; Pound in any case left it behind with that "bunch of goups" who shared his belief in the non-discursive image — which presented, as he put it, "an intellectual and emotional complex in an instant of time" — but were, in his view, too lazy to follow his injunction against the 'superfluous word'; and he developed the aesthetic of the Image in his own way. But he continued to avow his debt to the French poets and critics — to Gautier of course, as well as to the later Symbolists, and Gourmont especially — and when he claims to have constructed a conscious aesthetic to fill the place of Rimbaud's intuitions he is (perhaps unconsciously) paraphrasing a claim made by Symons. For Rimbaud was the great proof of the authenticity of the Romantic dream, and the general validity of the arbitrary symbols of the interior landscape. Pound knew this, as a modern poet should. T. E. Hulme, perhaps, did not.

Hulme was, in some respects, the most influential of the *cénacle*, and he made the principal attempt to give its image-theory a proper philosophical backing. His influence continues to be considerable, but it is frequently misunderstood for the reason, mainly, that he himself proclaimed a war against Romanticism; and this proclamation has more or less drowned the truth that his whole attitude is intelligible only on the assumption that his thought derives, with no fundamental variation, from the historical theory of the Image and the related tradition of the necessary isolation of the artist. It is specially important to get this right, because on it largely depends the relevance of what I have to say later about post-Hulmian criticism. This is not to deny Hulme's importance or his centrality, which I think has to be affirmed in spite of Pound's rejection of him, and although Eliot was not much affected by him until his posthumous period of influence began with the publication of *Speculations* in 1924. It is true that the important things brought together in Hulme's mind were available elsewhere; still, he brought them together, and people took note of the way he put them. But I do not think I can establish Hulme's connexion with my subject without giving a summary account of his thought, with some comment.

This is easy enough to do, because Hulme hardly got past the planning stage; had he lived, it is improbable that it would have been so easy to see all round his thought and observe what is wrong with it. As it is, the collection of essays, lectures and notes which go under the title of *Speculations* (edited by Herbert Read), supplemented by the additional material printed by Michael Roberts in his study of 1938, and by a few uncollected essays from *The New Age*, is a manageable and fairly lucid corpus. (More material has recently been announced for publication, but is not yet available). I restate the leading ideas only because it seems to me that at any rate one aspect of their historical significance has not emerged in previous explanations. One might summarise it in this way. Hulme hands over to the English tradition a modernised, but essentially traditional, aesthetic of Symbolism. It would have made ground here in any case, but Hulme gave it a form which has persisted into modern thought, a form which for various reasons offers an acceptable version of the magic Image, or Romantic anti-positivism, and of the excluded artist. The hostility of Pound (his insistence that Ford rather than Hulme was the dominant figure of the pre-war group) is explained by Pound's dislike of the metaphysics adhering to the Hulmian theory — a metaphysics which has had its own considerable success, and in fact grew up side by side with Symbolist aesthetics. Pound's own aesthetic is not fundamentally different from Hulme's, though he is quite right to insist that it was available to him without Hulme's mediation.

The easiest way to explain Hulme is to follow, for a while at any rate, in his own wake. This means putting the metaphysics first, and the general theory of the history of art, though it is tolerably certain that he must have worked out a theory of the Image first and put together the rest of his theory afterwards. Hulme was not, we are told, a Roman Catholic; but he had strong Catholic sympathies. He was a devoted admirer of Bergson, whose *Introduction to Metaphysics* he translated. He had a great veneration for Pascal; and when we name Pascal and Bergson and add the name of Worringer, we have the triple source of Hulme's philosophy at any rate in so far as it affects his views on art.

To consider Bergson first: we are so accustomed (largely on the strength of the extraordinary celebrity of the paper called 'Romanticism and Classicism') to regard Hulme as a classicising, anti-Romantic thinker, that we incline to ignore his strong affiliation to that organicist, anti-positivist stream of ideas that stems from the Romantic movement. From Bergson Hulme derives the concept of discontinuity in nature, the notion of the 'intensive manifold' which is the philosophical justification of his theory of the image; and also his view of the artist as a man deficient in the normal human orientation to action. In Bergson the concept of discontinuity relates to the absolute lack of commerce between the mechanical and the vital, the former being the concern of the 'exact' sciences, against which art in the modern world is always more or less on the defensive; the second, not available to the intellect but only to 'intuition', is the business of a special class of enquirers, and these are artists. To these two discontinuous zones of truth Hulme adds another, borrowed from an earlier anti-naturalist, Pascal. The third order is a realm of absolute ethical and religious values, and it assumes a considerable though occasionally ambiguous importance in Hulme's theories. By definition it is utterly dissimilar to the other two realms, mechanical and vital, though Hulme himself held (and there are apparent contradictions in his thought on the point) that it was, if possible, more like the mechanical than the vital in at least one respect; it was absolutely unrelated to the vital, completely abstract. At this point Hulme professes his pleasure at having the support of Husserl and G. E. Moore, whom he treats as virtually neo-scholastic philosophers.

The second creditor is the German aesthetician Worringer. His thesis, *Abstraktion und Einfühlung*, was published in 1908 (a belated English translation is now available, published by Messrs. Routledge and Kegan Paul in 1953) and Hulme must have been one of its earliest English readers. Its basic ideas, which are all reported in *Speculations*, stem from a sudden perception that the theory of empathy as formulated by Theodor Lipps applies only to some kinds of art. "Just as the urge to empathy as a pre-assumption of aesthetic experience finds its gratification in the beauty of the organic, so the urge to abstraction finds its beauty in the life-denying organic." 'Life-denying' and 'life-alien' are key-words in Worringer. They apply to the kind of art produced by primitive peoples and in all phases of civilisation characterised by a fear of the world, by spiritual agoraphobia. Of the primitive he says "it is because he stands so lost and spiritually helpless amidst the things of the eternal world, because he experiences only obscurity and caprice in the inter-connection and flux of the phenomena of the external world, that the urge is so strong in him to divest the things of the external world of their caprice and obscurity and to impart to them a value of necessity and a value of regularity." So the primitive makes an abstract quasi-geometrical art, emancipated "from all the contingency and temporality of the world-picture". If you compare Egyptian art with Greek you find the first life-alien and the second life-worshipping, the first abstract and the other dependent on empathy. Compare Byzantine with Renaissance art and you have the same polarity. The Renaissance was pantheistic life-worship, it had an "unproblematical sense of being at home in the world"; man had mastered nature, and there was no mystery to be afraid of, so that art became a means of "objectified self-enjoyment". It therefore replaced an art that was abstract (in Worringer's very wide sense) and non-organic. Worringer does not deny "joy at the new possibilities of felicity" created by the Renaissance, but laments "the great values hallowed by an immense tradition that were lost forever with this victory of the organic, of the natural".

Hulme was more uncompromising. Accepting the view that the Renaissance represents a prime historical crisis, he claimed also that the *Weltanschauung* it introduced had remained dominant until his own time (for both he and Worringer, like nearly all serious Romantic thinkers, imagined themselves to be living at a moment of historical crisis, after which, in their case, a more primitive, more abstract art was to replace the Renaissance tradition of humanism and empathy) and that this *Weltanschauung* was entirely bad. The typical philosophical decision of the Renaissance for Hulme was the exclusion from serious consideration of the dogma of Original Sin; this gone (as Pascal saw) the whole third estate of value was closed, because perfection had to be conceived in entirely human terms;

from this follows a radical change in art (for Hulme the Renaissance had no religious art at all) and in philosophy (which becomes consistently anthropocentric and anti-religious). If life, specifically human life, is at the centre, any attempt to think ethically must result in a confusion of the human and the divine. This confusion is the direct cause of relativism in ethics, modernism in religion, and Romanticism in literature. Romanticism is merely a phase of Renaissance Pelagianism, a humanistic sham religion ("spilt religion" in his most famous phrase, because of its weakness and shapelessness by comparison with the categorical form of absolute ethics).

Hulme set great store by his historical theories, holding that the main object of such speculations was the important one of destroying false categories in modern thought: a proposition which the author of a study like this, aimed ultimately at the same object, must heartily endorse. He undertook to make good this theory of the Renaissance by an elaborate examination of the philosophies of the period; and it is clear that had he had time to do so he must have modified his general theory with some severity; like the Romantics he so fiercely assailed, he did not know enough. A critique of this aspect of his historical theory would be irrelevant to the present purpose; it is sufficient for the moment to insist that Hulme was one of the first of the English to discover, what was later to become a dominating concept in modern criticism, some kind of disastrous psychical shift, some original moral catastrophe, in human history about the time of the Renaissance, and to couple it with a belief that another crisis, another major alteration of sensibility, was at hand. For a critique of this extremely important and characteristic Symbolist historical doctrine, the reader is referred to the following Chapter.

For Hulme, the epoch of humanism, anti-religious in every department of life, but visibly so in art, was ending. He lavishes his contempt upon it; with a sort of doctrinaire fury he eliminates as bad and anti-religious (because on the side of life) even Michelangelo. Nor does he care for the kind of thing other Roman Catholics like — Fra Angelico, for instance. His Catholicism is intellectual in the extreme, almost to the point of being a dogmatic abstract from the religion; without its support he cannot have the world-picture he wants, but he will have none of its tenderness and sentiment. The art he cares for is that of the period which the Renaissance ended, an epoch which believed in Original Sin and produced, at its best, a geometric art quite distinct from the vitalism of Renaissance art, which ministered to the spectator's pleasure in being alive, his desire to be *acting*. The art of Byzantium abhors all this, being concerned with absolute non-human values; being life-alien, remote from organic life and even detesting it. This art resembled not that humanist art which began in Athens, but Egyptian religious sculpture and the art of primitive peoples. Geometrical abstraction is a characteristic of cultures which understand the human lot as tragic, and distinguish sharply between the human and the divine, never confusing them, as the 'vitalist' art he hated did. Hulme applies to philosophies and art alike what he calls his *critique of satisfaction*. Never mind what the philosophers say, he advises; ask instead, what emotional requirement in themselves are they trying to satisfy. And all post-Renaissance philosophy is the same, so considered; it satisfies only the need for an assurance of human centrality. But new needs are now, he adds, appearing, and we are beginning, with Epstein and Wyndham Lewis, to get that anti-vitalist, geometric art of which the beginnings were to be perceived in Cézanne.

Whenever Hulme generalises about historical periods he goet wrong. The critique of satisfaction apparently fails to distinguish between Descartes and Schopenhauer, and it tells us that Hartley and the later Coleridge were seeking the same answers. It is impossible to understand how anybody who had read the *Essay on Man* could possibly regard Pope as exempt from the heresy (which Hulme called 'Romantic') of denying the *absolute* inaccessibility of ethics to the reason; Pope's trace of scepticism has very little to do with the chilly fideism of Hulme, and he has far more of Montaigne than Pascal in him. Much more important than the numerous minor objections of this sort that one could bring against Hulme is the well-established fact (ably presented in Michael Roberts's book) that he disastrously misrepresents Romantic philosophy. For Hulme, as we have seen, Romanticism was a calamity however you looked at it: politically, philosophically, aesthetically. It was the anthropocentric assumption of the Renaissance at the stage of mania, all Rousseauistic rubbish about personality, progress and freedom, all a denial of human limit and imperfection. (In fact it would be truer to say that the movement was obsessed by Original Sin than to say, as Hulme does, that it completely ignored it, and made life the measure of all values). For Hulme, as for all seers, the moment at which he was thinking was the perfect one for seeing the whole matter in perspective, and so breaking history into two parts (Augustine to the Renaissance, the Renaissance to Hulme). He did not even see how inconsistent he was about Coleridge, whose 'vital' he sometimes uses in its original Coleridgean sense, and sometimes in Worringer's sense, with great confusion — a confusion, incidentally, which reflects the Paterian life-and-death ambiguity which we have already looked at, and which turns up again in the aesthetic of Vortex. Nor did he see how dependent he was upon the tradition he was attacking, despite his avowed and enormous debt to Bergson. In so far as he was merely doing propaganda for a new abstract art which had already got under way he was primarily a reporter of Worringer, and that is consistent and defensible as far as it goes, which is not so far as the main historical generalisation; but in so far as he was introducing a new 'classical' poetry — anti-humanist poetry he means, which is a pretty paradox in itself — his position is complex and unsatisfactory, because he has not found out what it really is. We shall see more clearly where he stood if we consider the theory of the image which is central to his whole aesthetic. It is closely related to the concept of discontinuity, with its attendant rejection of empathic, *vital* art; but, as we shall see, it fits much more neatly into the old Romantic-Symbolist theory with its dualist implication (*two* discontinuous orders related to reason and imagination) than into the triplex structure of his own Bergsonian-Pascalian hypothesis.

Let us, then, look at Hulme's requirements for good poetry. Negatively, it must not be concerned with the myth of human perfection or perfectibility in any form; it must accept the strict limitations of human powers, be life-alien. (Note that Hulme is evasive and inconsistent about Coleridge's Imagination, fearing that there is some connection between it and the hated divinisation of human intellect that denies limit; he seems to have been unaware of the controlling force over Coleridge's thought of his refusal to give up the doctrine of Original Sin, whatever metaphysical labour this refusal might involve him in. In fact Hulme's 'intellect' is much the same as the Coleridgean and Wordsworthian 'reason', the reflective faculty that partakes of death.) The acceptance of limit will at once cut out the ecstatic meaning and hysterical aspiration Hulme regards as characteristic of Romantic poetry. The first positive requirement is for *precise description* (Hulme might have reflected that it is also the first requirement of Wordsworth's *Preface* of 1815). For Hulme, however, this precision concerns the recording of images; and here we are at the core of Hulmian aesthetics.

Without pausing to comment upon its deficiencies, let us look at Hulme's distinction between prose and verse.

In prose as in algebra concrete things are embodied in signs or counters which are moved about according to the rules, without being visualised at all in the process. There are in prose certain type situations and arrangements of words, which move as automatically into certain other arrangements as do functions in algebra. One only changes the X's and the Y's back into physical things at the end of the process. Poetry, in one aspect at any rate, may be considered as an effort to avoid this characteristic of prose. It is not a counter language, but a visible concrete one. It is a compromise for a language of intuition which would hand over sensations bodily. It always endeavours to arrest you, and to make you continuously see a physical thing, to prevent you gliding through an abstract process. It chooses fresh epithets and fresh metaphors, not so much because they are new, and we are tired of the old, but because the old cease to convey a physical thing and become abstract counters. A poet says a ship 'coursed the seas' to get a physical image, instead of the counter word 'sailed'. Visual meanings can only be transferred by the new bowl of metaphor; prose is an old pot that lets them leak out. Images in verse are not mere decoration, but the very essence of an intuitive language.

Presumably no one would now accept this as it is put; the semantics is, to say the least, naive, and Hulme's emphasis on the visual quality of all images (though not his insistence on their physical quality) has been outgrown. But that "images are the very essence of an intuitive language" is as much an assumption of modern criticism as of Coleridge's. Poetry, by

127

virtue of the image, *is*; prose merely describes. One is end, the other means. What poetry seems to be *about* is therefore irrelevant to its value. "Subject doesn't matter." Poetry is bad when it directs the attention away from the physical uniqueness and oneness of the image (the poem itself of course is an image, if it is good) and enables the reader "to glide through an abstract process". It is concrete, because the Image can be represented only as concrete, and entirely devoid of discursive meanings and appeals to the intellect; it is the direct representation of what is intuited. Whether the poem is good or not depends upon the accuracy of the representation, and upon that alone.

> I always think that the fundamental process at the back of all the arts might be represented by the following metaphor. You know what I call architect's curves — flat pieces of wood with all different kinds of curvature. By a suitable selection from these you can draw approximately any curve you like. The artist I take to be a man who simply can't bear the idea of that 'approximately'. He will get the exact curve of what he sees whether it be an object or an idea in the mind.

Poems are concerned with intuited truth, not with what is discursively explicable by the reason. The mechanical can be measured in its own way, but the approximations which are all that way can offer in the aesthetic sphere are intolerable to the artist.

But this does not mean that good poems are about 'the infinite' or 'the ineffable' — that would be to fall into the Romantic heresy in a slightly different form. We return to Bergson's two orders. What *is* intuited in terms of the Image? In what circumstances does this act of intuition occur? Hulme's answer is Bergson's. The sphere in which intuition operates is that reality which is conceived "as a flux of interpenetrated elements unseizable by the intellect". What normally debars our entry into this sphere is the usual orientation of the human mind towards action. If that were not so we should have easy commerce with it, and there would be no need for art at all; as it is, the artist is "a man who is emancipated from the ways of perception engendered by action".

At this stage in the book it is hardly necessary to point out how richly 'Romantic' this formulation of the artist's function is, but it is worth emphasising that the twin concepts of isolation and image occur in Hulme as surely as in the poetry he despised. But we must return to the question of the intuited image.

Hulme's metaphysical justification of his image-theory is borrowed from Bergson. The human intellect tends to explain (*explico*, unfold) everything in a manner fitting its limitations; it analyses, because "that is the only way in which the intellect can deal with things"; "we reduce everything to extensive manifolds". We unfold everything out in space, and we tend to think that everything that cannot be so unfolded must be unknowable. But of course this is not so, and anybody can think of things which are somehow known but resist this form of knowing them. How do such things differ from the others which allow themselves to be treated as extensive manifolds? Bergson argues that such things, "while incomprehensible by our ordinary standards" are nevertheless finite. The nature of their complexity is qualitative, not quantitative; they simply do not yield to explanation, to discursive methods of analysis; they resist the intellect. Their parts are "interpenetrated in such a manner that they could not be separated or analysed out". And yet one should not even speak of parts, because the complex thing is a continuous whole, and it is impossible to conceive of its parts as having a separate existence. This is the intensive manifold, by the very terms of the argument impossible to define; it is accessible only to intuition, belonging to a different order of reality. It is "indescribable but not unknowable". The artist knows it; it is his Image. It is finite; hence the need for precision. Its meaning is the same thing as its form, and the artist is absolved from participation with the discursive powers of the intellect.

This theory, as Hulme explains it, makes a show of being in opposition to Romantic imprecision — hence the emphasis on finiteness, and the lack of reference to the third, Pascalian order — but in fact it is fundamentally a new statement of the old defence of poetry against positivism and the universe of death. It is a revised form of the old proclamation that poetry has special access to truth, and is not merely light entertainment for minds tired out by physics. Poets, excluded from action, are enabled to achieve the special form of cognition and pierce the veil and intuit truth; this is communicated in the Image.

And yet 'new' is certainly the wrong word for all this. Hulme himself recognises the essential similarity between his intuited manifold and Schopenhauer's Idea, arguing reasonably for the technical superiority of the later conception. And this similarity, from which Hulme draws no conclusion, is in a sense the key to a proper historical appraisal of Hulme on poetry. Bergson himself is the almost inevitable result of the nineteenth-century effort to find room for art amid the encroachments of science; and the aesthetic of the Symbolists is predominantly the artists's version of such anti-intellectualist concepts as the Idea of Schopenhauer. Hulme knew de Gourmont, but avoided his conclusion that the alternative to intellect was something more primitive; he avoids anything remotely resembling surrealism, and for the *rêve* so dear to Symbolism he substitutes his rather austere version, a higher but finite order of truth. To this extent there is justice in his claim that he is at war with Romantic imprecision; but it must be said that the term *rêve* covers many meanings, including that of a means of access to realms of truth habitually inaccessible, and Hulme's artist is really the Romantic *voyant* expressed in terms more agreeable to a man who disliked some kinds of philosophical language. Insist as he might on the *finite* nature of his intuited truth, it is only another version of that truth unavailable to science which was part of the whole protest against eighteenth-century 'uniformitarianism' (whether expressed as German 'organicism' or as something more characteristically English in the thought of Blake and Coleridge). To get the exact curve of the thing, insisting upon the imperviousness to paraphrase of the symbolic work of art (the 'aesthetic monad') was Mallarmé's business as much as Hulme's; in fact Mallarmé anticipates Hulme in various particulars, such as the theory that a poem must be read silently, and both writers were driven (Hulme in *Cinders*, his 'Notes for a new *Weltanschauung*') to the dance as a necessary emblem of the symbol. In short, the Hulmian Image — precise, orderly, anti-discursive, the product of intuition — is the Symbol of the French poets given a new philosophical suit. As a matter of aesthetic decency it may be that this was needed; but once it is granted that Hulme was trying to do much the same thing as Mallarmé, it becomes evident that he did not do it very well.

As I have said, Hulme falls instinctively into the image of the Dancer, and to complete the pattern he writes in 'Notes on Language and Style' of "the beauty of the feminine form. . . as a typical vesture or symbol of beauty herself", adding that

> Rossetti saw the spiritual element in face and form, and desired the spirit through his desire for the body, and at last did not know the one desire from the other, and pressed on, true mystic that he was, in ever-narrowing circles, to some third thing that seemed to lie behind both desires. 'Soul is form and doth the body make.'

The prose here is in the Paterian tradition, quite unlike Hulme's usual colloquial brightness; it could be Yeats. The quotation from a Renaissance poet (Spenser) is a borrowing from the enemy; Hulme must have realised, with his predecessors and successors, that there was matter in such poetry made to his hand (compare the vogue for Donne's passage on Elizabeth Drury). And the reference to Rossetti is surely significant. In matter and manner this short passage is pure Romantic. And Hulme was certainly sufficiently informed by *l'âme romantique* to see the affinity of his kind of thinking about poetry for mysticism and magic. He calls the Christian mystics "analogous to his own temper" (he would have been interested in the modern theory that much seventeenth-century poetry is technically based on prescribed methods of meditation) and he admires the "physical analogies" of the Neo-Platonists, which are in the end the *correspondance* of Baudelaire and the Magic of Yeats. Something of the sort is, of course, necessary to any Symbolist theory of poetry, for if you insist on calling paraphrase a heresy, if you insist that the common language of reason cannot achieve knowledge of the thing that the Image is, then you are forced to guard against the absolute surrender of the power of communicating by some theory explaining how your supra-rational knowledge can be shared. Hulme has not the Great Memory, and he has no theory of shared subliminal symbolisms; nor has he the modern veneration for the magic underworld of language, to be visited by all who can achieve the golden bough of a pun or an irony. Instead he has the Bergsonian Veil which the artist can pierce, to show what everybody could see if only they were likewise equipped. It is a High Dream perhaps, but a dream all the same; and the view that under certain conditions everybody can dream it is a magical view.

Hulme remained committed to this view so long as he persisted in his opinion of language as — in poetry — a mode of communicating *visual* images, "a compromise for a language of intuition — to make you continuously see a physical thing"; the poet strictly as *voyant*. There seems no doubt that the next step forward in Romantic aesthetic depended upon a new theory of language. Hulme was very deficient here, though there are possibilities in his work of a development which have rendered superfluous the awkward implications of the view he professed. The problem was to preserve the Symbol (the 'aesthetic monad', the Image alogical yet meaningful, or as Sir Herbert Read has recently called it, 'the poetic Gestalt') and yet to be rid of magic. This could not be done so long as the Image was thought of as a thing seen only, or so long as language was considered as a means of handing over visual concreteness only. In his anxiety to distinguish between symbolic and non-symbolic language Hulme commits himself absolutely to this visual hypothesis. His Symbol is a visual thing, and its opposite is just the dead sign of an abstract prose process. Professor Lehmann has pointed out very similar vagaries in earlier Symbolist attempts at a theory of language; Hulme's peculiar interests make his different, but only in detail.

In fact the next step forward was taken by I. A. Richards, apparently approaching the problem from a very different angle, though soon drawn into the Coleridgean sphere of influence, and near enough to Hulme to feel the need of criticising him. There is even a sense in which, without too much paradox, one might call Richards a follower of Hulme, despite the formal rejection in *The Philosophy of Rhetoric*. Hulme would surely have come to see the force of this assault on his view of language as a collection of signs with limited reference, and to enjoy the idea of language as itself a series of 'interpenetrating contexts' (the very sphere of existence of the Symbol) and seen how directly this development is related to the theory of 'interpenetrating reality' involved in his concept of the intensive manifold. In a way — as I think Professor Lehmann has seen — Richards provides Symbolist aesthetic with a belated theory of language. If one considers the Richard view of *total meanings* (meanings determined by *form*, not *sign*) one sees how close it comes to such a provision; and the unfortunate 'pseudo-statement' is after all merely the Image looked at from a disapproving positivist point of view. Another point: the early psychology of Richards, with its picture of the attitudes induced by aesthetic means as not conducing to, or as inhibited from action, is Hulmian and Bergsonian; in fact, its roots go even deeper into Romantic thought, as I have suggested. In Richards we encounter in a very strange new guise not only the Image but also the ingrained anti-didacticism and the hostility to action which informed the tradition as Hulme also knew it.

All this is, however, a little outside my terms of reference, and I return to less linguistic conceptions of the Image, and the other members of Hulme's circle.

About the least satisfactory aspect of Imagism proper is the implication of absolute stillness in the Imagine; and the doctrine of Vortex overcomes this. I imagine the origins of Vorticism will not be fully understood until the Pound-Yeats relationship is better known, but it is not unreasonable to guess that the term derived in the first place from the Empedoclean vortex which attracted Yeats because it provided a magical symbol of the resolution between antinomies like concord-discord, life-death, stillness-movement. The Vortex is the Image in movement, though paradoxically still: "our Vortex desires the immobile rythm (sic) of its switftness". This appealed to Yeats because of his fascination with oscillation between opposites, to Pound because he had abondoned simple Imagism (which gave concreteness but not vitality and action) and to Wyndham Lewis, who was interested in the painter's problem of movement (like Wilde in the dialogue I have quoted) but saw how destructive, and indeed absurd, were some contemporary efforts to solve it. He rejected Futurism as simply offering a series of static images and asking one to accept them as moving, which is possible in time because of the retina's retaining powers. Of course this was for Lewis no answer at all, and he provides instead another version, very curious and with the appearance of originality, of the old paradox of the Image as life-in-death, movement-in-stillness, with a strong infusion of Hulmian metaphysics which nevertheless professes to exclude

133

Bergson. "Deadness. . . is the first condition of art"; but it is the deadness of the still centre of the Vortex.

Wyndham Lewis has belatedly become the subject of serious investigation, particularly by Mr. Geoffrey Wagner, who has published some good papers on the Vorticist aesthetic, including one which demonstrates Lewis's heavy debt to the Bergson he so often blasted. It may consequently seem dangerous, in a perfunctory allusion like this, to declare that the doctrine is a normal development of Romantic thought, particularly as it is always, as for instance by Pound, referred to as a classicising movement. Yet the Vorticist artist is an individual exceptionally endowed to know truth by a special mode of cognition; the images he seeks are "radiant nodes or clusters, from which and through which, and into which, ideas are constantly rushing" — and these are the images the Romantic poet has always sought. The Image is a 'concrete manifestation', and 'ideas' rush in and out of it, but it is not in itself discursive, and cannot mean anything except what it is. It is absolute, concrete, thought-and-image, life-in-death. We cannot help thinking of Pater and Wilde; and, honestly enough, the first issue of BLAST, in the section on its own ancestry, acknowledges Pater as aforebear: "All arts approach the condition of music (sic)". "Vortex is energy", but deadness is the first condition of art: "Our Vortex does not suck up to life". What is sought is an image which is "a sort of death and silence in the middle of life", having absolutely no connexion with the 'vital' (Worringer's sense). Lewis, like Yeats, was much interested in mummies, "the egyptian *living death*", which is 'vital' because it is art "unimpeded," in Mr. Wagner's phrase, "by the fluxes of life". This is, surely, the old paradox, as we found it in 'Emerald Uthwart'. Life is rejected because of its divorce of spirit and sense; "the lines and masses of the statue are its soul". It isn't a machine driven by "a little egoistic fire inside"; rather it "lives soullessly and deadly by its frontal lines and masses". This may be a programme for abstraction, but it cannot avoid saying that the Image *lives;* there is the Hulmian ambiguity about 'vitality'. The work of art has to *live*, but differently; the difference from ordinary modes of life is so great that one can say it is dead: "dead, yet flesh and bone". The rejection of 'life' is made, as usual, in the interests of a higher kind of life and truth. The dead image has life, in the sense of Yeats's dictum, that being is possessed only by the dead, and with the implication that this life is of a different and higher order than organic life. The Image inhabits the Yeatsian Byzantium with its marvellous permanent vitality; it is abstract as Yeats's statues are abstract, which, with their drilled eyeballs and blank faces, "moved or seemed to move in marble or in bronze". And in one curious expression in the first BLAST we encounter our emblematic Dancer; again, as in Hulme's lines on Rossetti, we sense the incongruous movement of ninetyish prose in these brisk and brash pages: "Our Vortex will not hear of anything but its disastrous polished dance".

In one other way Vorticism betrays its affiliation to the tradition of which Hulme was the important contemporary representative. This is in its teaching concerning the place of the artist in an active world. BLAST, we may recall, made its two appearances just before and just after the outbreak of the 1914 war, so that the question of action was more than usually acute. It decided that the Vorticist "cannot have to the full the excellent and efficient qualities we admire in the man of action unless he eschews action and sticks hard to thought". So the account given of the artist's position, like that of the Image itself, is fully Romantic.

So much (and it is scarcely enough) for Vortex; a word now for Ezra Pound. The principles of the Imagist manifesto ('direct treatment of the thing', avoidance of abstract language, exclusion of superfluous words and abandonment of metronomic rhythms) are all Hulmian, the last of them relating to his theory of free verse (one can't get the exact curve of the thing with prefabricated rhythms). Yet according to Pound himself, Hulme's connexion with Imagism and, more important, with Pound's independent aesthetic development, was nugatory. He expressly states, in an essay reprinted by Mr. Hugh Kenner in his *Poetry of Ezra Pound*, that "the critical light during the years immediately pre-war in London shone not from Hulme but from Ford", though he adds that the essays collected in *Speculations* "may have come later as a Godsend".

The reason for this disclaimer is, to put it simply, that whereas Ford "knew about WRITING", Hulme spent his time on "crap like Bergson", and had given up poetry. Pound claimed that he himself directed Hulme's attention to the significance of the difference between the language of Caval-canti, who hands over sensations bodily, and that of Petrarch, which is "fustian and ornament". But, alas, Hulme was "trying to be a philosopher", and consequently he went into the meta-physics of such distinctions, whereas to Pound this was merely taking the argument where it was of no use to anybody. For Pound the problem begins and ends with the establishing of the genuine thing-ness of the image; he wants *things*, not ideas. So the ideogram as he learned it from Fenellosa was a boon to him. It was constructed not of ideas but of things; it had no intellectual content whatever, and it did not discourse. In so far as the *Cantos* contrive to be an assemblage of ideograms in a significant relation to each other, and nothing else (of course they do not entirely succeed in this, as he admits) they are one vast image. They are, in fact, the only kind of long poem the Symbolist aesthetic will admit. It should be clear that Pound's ideogram is yet another variety of the Romantic Image, and that he could have prepared himself for Fenellosa's revelations without having known Hulme at all. What Fenellosa did was to convince him that one could have the Symbolist Image without having Schopenhauer or Bergson or indeed any other Western philosopher; that the Chinese had an analogous symbol without metaphysical trappings. Pound could not have seen the point of the ideogram for European poetry if he had not been schooled in the Romantic Image. And he admits this influence, though minimising it.

What it comes to in the end is that Pound, like Hulme, like Mallarmé and many others, wanted a theory of poetry based on the non-discursive *concetto*. In varying degrees they all obscurely wish that poetry could be written with something other than words, but since it can't, that words may be made to have the same sort of physical presence "as a piece of string". The resistance to words in their Image is explained by the fact that words are the means of a very different sort of com-munication; they are so used to being discursive that it is almost impossible to stop them discoursing.

This linguistic difficulty has been tackled very seriously since Hulme's day, and certainly it is enough in itself to provoke radical criticism of the whole tradition. Should it invariably be deplored that poems tend to 'say' something? There is that tell-tale 'binding-matter', as Pound calls it, in the *Cantos*. Yeats, untroubled by the stricter theoretical limitations, makes no bones about having plenty of binding-matter, and criticises the *Cantos* in terms I have already alluded to. Are they really like a fugue, as their author says, he asks, or are they a great poem smothered in its own technical presumptuousness? Pound's answer is in a letter of 1937: "If Yeats knew a fugue from a frog he might have transmitted what I told him in some way that would have helped rather than obfuscated his readers". But the ways in which words can resemble music are limited (particularly fugal music) and there is now, I imagine, little confidence in the ultimate clarity of Pound's poem. The most interesting thing about his musical analogy is that it is musical for precisely the reasons that Pater and Verlaine had already given; the *Cantos* aspire to the condition of music because music is all form and no discourse. Hulme avoids this analogy because of his preoccupation with visual form, but this is an insignificant difference between them. Nothing that either says is essentially different from what has been said many times before, and neither provides for the great need, a correction to the Symbolist theory of language.

This attempt to place Hulme and his friends in the full Romantic tradition may have succeeded only in convincing the reader that he has (in this place) been paid disproportionate attention. But Hulme stands conveniently between the generation of Symons and our own time; and, what is more, his influence has proved hardy. It remains perceptible in the American 'New' Criticism; it plays its part in the work of the younger Poundian critics of the present moment; even as far afield as Japan, I notice, there is a Hulmian movement. For what he owed to the past, and for what his successors have taken from him (without, as I think, fully understanding the history of what they had got) he demands attention. The next chapter is in part concerned with his later influence, as I bring nearer the present day the history of the Romantic Image. And, as I shall have to start by considering the very striking success of a Symbolist theory of literary history, it is worth remarking that Hulme was the first Englishman — before even Yeats — to develop such a theory. Later it became the doctrine of 'dissociation of sensibility'.

137

VIII

'DISSOCIATION OF SENSIBILITY'
MODERN SYMBOLIST READINGS
OF LITERARY HISTORY

> The primary pigment of poetry is the IMAGE.
> BLAST
>
> The poetic myths are dead; and the poetic image,
> which is the myth of the individual, reigns in their
> stead.
>
> C. DAY LEWIS

WHEN the accounts come to be rendered, it may well appear to future historians that the greatest service done by early twentieth-century criticism to contemporary poetry has been this: it has shown poets a specially appropriate way of nourishing themselves from the past. It has shown them that their isolation, and their necessary preoccupation with the Image, do not cut them off from all their predecessors, and that there are ways of looking at the past which provide valuable insights into essentially modern possibilities and predispositions. The need was to bring literary history — and this involved other kinds of history too — to the support of the Image; to rewrite the history of poetry in Symbolist terms. The whole effort crystallised, in 1921, in Mr. Eliot's famous announcement of the doctrine of the dissociation of sensibility, and although this was by no means so original an idea as it has been called, it will necessarily be at the centre of what I have to say about this extremely important phase of my subject.

The doctrine has lately been wilting under well-directed criticism, though there is no doubt that it will continue, whether under the same name or not, whether fallacious or not, to exert a powerful influence for a long time yet. My business here is merely to establish that it has a strong connexion with the development, in the present century, of the theory of the Image, and to ask why it has had such success. What I say about its value as a key to literary history is really incidental to this.

Mr. Eliot first used the expression 'dissociation of sensibility' in an essay on 'The Metaphysical Poets' (1921), and his last recorded comment upon the theory is in his British Academy lecture on Milton (1947). The first passage, as printed in *Selected Essays*, runs like this: Mr. Eliot has been saying that the dramatic verse of the late Elizabethans and early Jacobeans "expresses a degree of development of sensibility which is not found in any of the prose. . . In Chapman especially there is a direct sensuous apprehension of thought, or a recreation of thought into feeling, which is exactly what we find in Donne. . ." He then compares a passage of Chapman's and one by Lord Herbert of Cherbury with bits of Tennyson and Browning, and comments:

The difference is not a simple difference of degree between poets. It is something which had happened to the mind of England between the time of Donne or Lord Herbert of Cherbury and the time of Tennyson and Browning; it is the difference between the intellectual poet and the reflective poet. Tennyson and Browning are poets, and they think; but they do not feel their thought as immediately as the odour of a rose. A thought to Donne was an experience; it modified his sensibility. When a poet's mind is perfectly equipped for its work, it is constantly amalgamating disparate experience; the ordinary man's experience is chaotic, irregular, fragmentary. The latter falls in love, or reads Spinoza, and these two experiences have nothing to do with each other, or with the noise of the typewriter or the smell of cooking; in the mind of the poet these experiences are always forming new wholes.

We may express the difference by the following theory: The poets of the seventeenth century, the successors of the dramatists of the sixteenth, possessed a mechanism of sensibility which could devour any kind of experience. They are

139

simple, artificial, difficult, or fantastic, as their predecessors were; no less nor more than Dante, Guido Cavalcanti, Guinicelli, or Cino. In the seventeenth century a dissociation of sensibility set in, from which we have never recovered; and this dissociation, as is natural, was aggravated by the influence of the most powerful poets of the century, Milton and Dryden.

Observe that there are certain qualifications for poetry described as operative *now*, though possessed by the poets of the seventeenth century and none since (until now?). There are other places in Mr. Eliot's earlier criticism which amplify this statement, but we will content ourselves with his last pronouncement on the subject:

> I believe that the general affirmation represented by the phrase 'dissociation of sensibility'. . . retains some validity; but. . . to lay the burden on the shoulders of Milton and Dryden was a mistake. If such a dissociation did take place, I suspect that the causes are too complex and profound to justify our accounting for the change in terms of literary criticism. All we can say is, that something like this did happen; that it had something to do with the Civil War; that it would be unwise to say it was caused by the Civil War, but that it is a consequence of the same cause which brought about the Civil War; that we must seek the causes in Europe, not in England alone; and for what these causes were, we may dig and dig until we get to a depth at which words and concepts fail us.

In this passage Mr. Eliot seems to be recommending, as a desideratum, what had in fact already been done; for by 1947 supplementary enquiries into the dissociation had long ceased to be conducted entirely in terms of literary criticism. Almost every conceivable aspect of seventeenth-century life had been examined by scholars anxious to validate the concept, though it is true that the investigators were usually historians of literature by profession. In very general terms it might be said that the notion of a pregnant historical crisis, of great importance in every sphere of human activity, was attractive because it gave design and simplicity to history; and because it explained in a subtly agreeable way the torment and division of modern life.

Feeling and thinking by turns, aware of the modern preference for intellect over imagination, a double-minded period measured itself by a serenely single-minded one. Poets tried again to be concrete, to charge their thinking with passion, to restore to poetry a truth independent of the presumptuous intellect. They looked admiringly to those early years of the seventeenth century when this was normal, and the scholars attended them with explanations of why it was so, and why it ceased to be so. There was, I think, an implicit parallel with the Fall. Man's soul, since about 1650, had been divided against itself, and it would never be the same again — though correct education could achieve something.

It is a measure of Mr. Eliot's extraordinary persuasiveness that thinkers in this tradition have for so long accepted the seventeenth century as the time of the disaster. As we see from his second pronouncement, he has himself stuck to this position, although he advises us to look back into earlier history for fuller explanations. Nor is his attitude difficult to understand; it is animated by a rich nostalgia for the great period of Anglican divinity, the period when the Church of England, beset on all sides by determined recusancy, confidently proposed itself as truly Catholic and apostolic — looking back, itself, to a vague past when the folly and arrogance of intellect had not yet begun the process of dissociating Christianity. This period ended with the Civil War, and the end of the first Anglo-Catholicism coincided with the end of an admired poetry and a great drama, both affected, to some extent, by ecclesiastically-determined attitudes, the drama remembering (but how faintly?) its devout origins, 'metaphysical poetry' the *concetto predicabile*. What happens is that the Civil War becomes a kind of allegory, with the Puritans as Pride of Intellect, and the King as Spiritual Unity.

The truth is that, if we look to Europe and not to England alone, we see that there was never much chance that the Church of England would be universally recognised as Catholic, and that 'something' had presumably 'happened' long before to predispose people against such recognition. And this is a characteristic situation. It is not merely a matter of wrong dates; however far back one goes one seems to find the symptoms of dissociation. This suggests that there is little historical propriety in treating it as a seventeenth-century event, even when the historian is serious and respectable enough not to assume that it really was an occurrence like, say, Pride's Purge, after which feeling disappeared from certain mental transactions, leaving a Rump of intellect with which we are still conducting our business. With more thoughtful chroniclers there is usually much emphasis on the dissociative force of science, and on the un-dissociated condition of pre-Baconian and pre-Cartesian philosophy and theology. But it is easy enough to show that scientists were already under Elizabeth incurring odium and the suspicion of atheism for a variety of reasons, all coming in the end to the charge that they were setting nature against God. Bacon's position with respect to religious laws that were apparently contrary to reason is very similar to that of many philosophers, especially those affected by Averroes and the great Aristotelian tradition of Padua, from the thirteenth century onward, to Pomponazzi in the early sixteenth and to Cremonini, an influential teacher who was, incidentally, a friend of that very Lord Herbert of Cherbury who was used as an example of the un-dissociated poet. Obviously the rediscovery of Aristotle involved in some sense a dissociation of Christian thought, tending ultimately to some such escape-device as the 'double-truth' of Averroism, first condemned, by a Church anxious to save rational theology, in the 1270s. And if we were to pursue the dissociation back into the past, we should find ourselves in Athens. Elizabethan 'atheism' was far more than a scientific issue; there was genuine anxiety, a real 'naturalist' movement widely affecting ethical and political conduct. Similarly, the condemnations of the 1270s referred not only to Averroism but to the book on love by Andreas Capellanus, and M. Gilson has spoken of "a sort of polymorphic naturalism stressing the rights of pagan nature" as characteristic of the period as a whole. It would be quite as reasonable to locate the great dissociation in the sixteenth or the thirteenth century as in the seventeenth; nor would it be difficult to construct arguments for other periods. The truth may be that we shall never find a state of culture worth bothering about (from the literary point of view, that is) in which language is so primitive as to admit no thinking that is not numinous; in which there is no possibility of a naturalist assault on the society's beliefs. The Christian 'West' has never wanted to be as primitive even as the Song of Solomon, and its whole immense allegorical tradition is the result of applying intellectual instruments to the dissection of writings in which thought and feeling are, if they are anywhere, inseparable.

But it seems to me much less important that there was not, in the sense in which Mr. Eliot's supporters have thought, a particular and far-reaching catastrophe in the seventeenth century, than that there was, in the twentieth, an urgent need to establish the historicity of such a disaster. And the attempt to answer the question why there should have been takes us back to the Image. The theory of the dissociation of sensibility is, in fact, the most successful version of a Symbolist attempt to explain why the modern world resists works of art that testify to the poet's special, anti-intellectual way of knowing truth. And this attempt obviously involves the hypothesis of an age which was different, an age in which the Image was more readily accessible and acceptable.

When, in fact, the poets and aestheticians of the Image turn their attention to history, it is in search of some golden age when the prevalent mode of knowing was not positivist and anti-imaginative; when the Image, the intuited, creative reality, was habitually respected; when art was not permanently on the defensive against mechanical and systematic modes of enquiry. Since the order of reality postulated as the proper study of the poet tends, in one way or another, to be granted supernatural attributes, the ideal epoch is usually a religious one. Hence the medievalism of Byzantinism of Hulme and the Decadents, of Yeats and Henry Adams. Hulme, in particular — as we have seen — exposes the whole process; he has to go back, using Worringer as a guide, to a moment of crisis (using one that already existed for historians, but using it in a new way) and achieve the required antithesis between his two age (undissociated and dissociated) by treating all thought between the Renaissance and his own time as of a piece. It was partly because this obviously would not do that the date of the crisis was moved on to 1650. But everybody in the tradition was agreed that there must have been such a crisis; it was necessary to their aesthetic, and the only point of dispute was its date.

There is a passage, to which I have already referred, in Pound's *Make It New*, that illuminates this aspect of the problem.

When the late T. E. Hulme was trying to be a philosopher. .
and fussing about Sorel and Bergson. . . I spoke to him one
day of the difference between Guido's precise interpretative
metaphor, and the Petrarchian fustian and ornament, point-
ing out that Guido thought in accurate terms; that the
phrases correspond to definite sensations undergone. . .
Hulme took some time ever it in silence, and then finally
said: "That is more interesting than anything anyone ever
said to me. It is more intersting than anything I ever read
in a book".

The only aspects of this odd interchange that I want to discuss are those which are relevant to what I am trying to say
about the historiography of modern Symbolist aesthetics. One
is that Pound is describing Cavalcanti as a poet of the integral
image, and contrasting him with Petrarch, a poet of the orna-
mental image, the image appended to discourse, the flower
stuck in sand. In the one there is 'a unification of thought and
feeling'; in the other, a dissociation of them. Another is
Hulme's reaction to what Pound said. The general idea could
not have been unfamiliar to him; after all, it was the reason
why he was fussing about Bergson. But a man is never more
impressed by an argument than when it provides unexpected
support for opinions he already holds, and Hulme could not
have been less than charmed to discover that Petrarch, of all
people — the First Man of that Renaissance he blamed so
strenuously — already exhibited the symptoms of error that
characterised the period, whereas Cavalcanti, an older contemporary of Dante, habituated to the hallowed concept of
discontinuity, brought up on Original Sin, had precisely those
Imagist qualities, that reluctance to glide away into abstraction. which for Hulme was the index of true poetry. Somewhere
between Cavalcanti and Petrarch a dissociation of sensibility,
it would seem, had set in; and from it, Hulme was willing to
add, we have never recovered.

But we have now to remind ourselves that Mr. Eliot claimed
for the poets of the seventeenth century the very qualities of
Dante, Cavalcanti, and Cino, and believed that the dissociation
came after these later poets. It is not in the nature of the concept of dissasiation that it should occur at random intervals,
any more than it is of the Fall; only on some such theory as

Yeats's can it occur more than once. What are we to conclude from this confusion?

The fact is that Mr. Eliot's argument for a general dissociation that can be detected in art is meant to satisfy much the same need as Hulme's, and Yeats's. For Hulme, as we have seen, the Renaissance is the critical moment; men began to ignore the human limitations suggested by the doctrine of Original Sin, and nothing has been right since. Romanticism is just the new disease at the stage of mania. For Yeats the great moment in the present historical phase is 1550; for about a century before that there was a tense perfection, celebrated in some of his most splendid prose; but after that everything changed, art faced in the wrong direction, the artist became more and more an exile. In fact Yeats's history is written in terms of this doctrine, written in a world that offended him socially and imaginatively, a world of 'shopkeeping logicians', the very existence of which he had to explain by exhaustive glosses on every conceivable aspect of the idea of dissociation. My own belief is that Yeats's expression of the whole aesthetic-historical complex is by far the most satisfactory and, in terms of poetry, the most fruitful. But the immediate point is that all these writers search history for this critical moment, and because they share much the same poetic heritage, they are all looking for much the same kinds of rightness and wrongness in historical periods. They seek, in short, a historical period possessing the qualities they postulate for the Image: unity, indissociability; qualities which, though passionately desired, are, they say, uniquely hard to come by in the modern world. That poets and critics so diverse in personality as Pound, Hulme, Yeats and Eliot, should all have made such similar incursions into Symbolist historiography is testimony to the great pressure the idea of the Image has exerted in the formative phase of modern poetic. Mr. Eliot's attempt, distinguished from the others by the accident of his personal concerns in theology, is not essentially different from them. It has only been more successful, partly because of his prestige and persuasive force, partly perhaps because of the growing scholarly tendency to medievalise the Renaissance, so that a later date for the split became more acceptable.

The fact remains that Mr. Eliot's is the version that has had wide currency. Like the others, it is, as I have been trying to

145

show, quite useless historically. It will not do to say that it is partly true, or true in a way, as some people now claim. A once-for-all event cannot happen every few years; there cannot be, if the term is to retain the significance it has acquired, dissociations between the archaic Greeks and Phidias, between Catullus and Virgil, between Guido and Petrarch, between Donne and Milton. As a way of speaking about *periods* the expression is much less useful than even 'baroque'. At its worst, it is merely a way of saying which poets one likes, and draping history over them. At its best it is an interesting primitivism, looking for an unmodern virtue, not as the noble savage was sought in the impossibly remote past or in Tahiti, but in Christian Europe right up to some moment in, or shortly after, what is vaguely called the Renaissance. The most deplorable consequence of the doctrine is that the periods and poets chosen to illustrate it are bound to receive perverse treatment; you must misrepresent them if you propose to make them justify a false theory. If the theory helps to produce good poetry (as it did) this is not worth complaining about, provided that it dies when this work is accomplished. But this theory shows every sign of surviving, and it is therefore a matter of importance to show how it has distorted Donne and Milton, the two poets most affected by it. Once again, the astonishing degree of distortion imposed here is a measure of the power generated by the Image in modern poetic.

Milton and Donne have been involved in an unhappy relationship (existing only in the fantasies of historians) which has seemed to mean that one of them has to be occulted to enable the other to be lit. Milton was to be put out — though it may be noted that Mr. Eliot's change of opinion about Donne was followed by an upward revision of his estimate of Milton. At the time when Donne was being admired for thinking passionately, Milton was being despised for writing monuments to dead ideas in a dead language. Milton, self-conscious post-lapsarian that he was, obstinately thought and discoursed *about* feeling, divorcing the body and soul, the form and matter, of the image. Donne, writing before the same Fall, had his intellect at the tip of his senses.

Superficially this argument was attractive because it gave major status to an obscure poet whose diction was inartificial, even colloquial, and who lived in times supposed to be very like modern times, in that the established order was already being threatened by those 'naturalist' forces which eventually dissociated sensibility. There is, of course, a contradiction here: Donne is admired because he was deeply troubled by the new philosophy, and also because he was lucky enough to live just before it became really troublesome. There is also an error of fact: Donne alludes frequently enough to the 'new philosophy', but nobody who has examined these allusions in their context can seriously believe he was much put out by it, and considering his religious views it would indeed be surprising if he had been. It might have been useful to the dissociationist argument if somebody had been prepared to capitalise this point, by way of emphasising Donne's pre-dissociation status; but there seems to have been a heavy commitment to the view that Donne was important to modern poets because of the ways in which his world resembled theirs, as well as because it was completely different from theirs. As usual, the history is feeble. But pure criticism has had very similar difficulties: Miss Tuve's now famous demonstration that Donne's images have a logical, or at any rate a pseudo-logical function, was a direct affront to the basis of the theory he was a poet of the modern Image; but it can scarcely have surprised anybody who had read Donne open-eyed and seen how much he depends on dialectical conjuring of various kinds, arriving at the point of wit by subtle syllogistic misdirections, inviting admiration by slight but totally destructive perversities of analogue, which re-route every argument to paradox. Some of this Mr. Eliot perhaps felt when he prematurely prophesied the demise of Donne during the tercentenary celebrations of 1931, and showed how far he had gone towards excluding Donne from the category of unified sensibility, saying outright that in him "there is a manifest fissure of thought and sensibility". Donne is, to say the least, of doubtful value to the Symbolist theory — less use than the poetic and critical experiments of some of his European contemporaries might have been. At first glance, one might be excused for wondering how Donne ever got mixed up with the theory of dissociation; the explanation of course lies in nineteenth-century thought.

Mr. F. W. Bateson, in a very important critique of the theory, has noticed in passing how little separates Mr. Eliot's formula from the conventional nineteenth-century view, which he exemplifies by Stopford Brooke's opinion that the Restoration saw the end "of a poetry in which emotion always accompanied thought". And something like this view can in fact be found in Coleridge. But after Grosart's edition of 1872 some people were already noticing that Donne wrote poems in which the note of passion, the true voice of feeling, was audible despite the fact that they were love poems unpromisingly couched in terms of alchemy, astronomy and law. It was this discovery of the true voice of feeling in such surroundings that led to what was in effect a late Romantic glorification of Donne. This was contemporary with the Blake revival, the teaching of Pater, and finally with the assimilation of the parallel but more important phenomenon of French Symbolism — in short, with the emergence of the modern Image as it was understood by Symons (a great champion of Donne and the Jacobean drama), and those who came under his influence: Yeats, and later Pound and Eliot. One can watch the older thought-and-feeling formula developing from a Romantic into a characteristically Symbolist hypothesis. George Eliot, who knew Donne by the time she wrote *Middlemarch*, assumes like her master Wordsworth that the true voice comes from artists of higher organic sensibility than other men, but can write in that novel — doubtless unconscious of her role as critical pioneer — that the poet is "quick to discern", but also "quick to feel" because he possesses "a soul in which knowledge passes instantaneously into feeling, and feeling flashes back as a new organ of knowledge".

This period of transition is greatly illuminated in a paper recently published by Mr. J. E. Duncan in the *Journal of English and Germanic Philology*. Anyone who has used the Victorian editions upon which much of our reading in seventeenth-century poetry still depends must have occasionally felt that there was some hallucinatory resemblance between certain observations made by the enthusiastic clerical editors and those of Mr. Eliot. Mr. Duncan has collected a great deal of evidence to show, not only that Donne was well and truly revived long before Eliot's essays, and indeed Grierson's edition, but that even 70 years ago people were talking about the poet in what we recognise as the modern way. By 1911, Courthope, in his *History*, was already complaining that it had probably gone too far. Grierson's great edition of the following year was accepted as merely setting the seal on Donne's reputation. But what is more interesting than this mere setting back of the starting post is the terminology in which the Victorian critics, pleased with their rediscovery of the conceit and of hard-thinking poetry, devised in order to praise the Metaphysical poets. They speak of its intellectual cunning *and* its power of 'sensibility' and then, quite early, we find ourselves approaching, with a sort of unconscious inevitability, the modern formula which combines these two qualities as two sides of a coin. Grosart says that Crashaw's thinking "was so emotional as almost always to tremble into feeling"; Cowley's thought is "made to pulsate with feeling". Symons finds that Donne's "senses speak with unparalleled directness"; Schelling that Donne's contribution to the English lyric was "intellectualised emotion". Poets began to find Donne-like qualities in their own work; in so doing, Francis Thompson spoke of his own "sensoriness instinct with mind", and the parallel was supported by Symons and by Mrs. Meynell. The familiar comparison between the seventeenth and twentieth centuries began as early as 1900; after that it was easy to play the game of parallel poets, and both Brooke and Bridges were credited with resemblances to Donne. Gosse and Grierson alike saw the similarity between Donne and Baudelaire, and briefly hinted at the parallel between English-Jacobean and French-Symbolist which was later to prove so fertile. Arthur Symons in fact developed the parallel to a considerable extent; he is the link between nineteenth- and twentieth-century orthodoxies of the Image, and of Donne and the seventeenth century.

Long before the great edition of Grierson, which made Donne relatively easy to read, and long before Mr. Eliot's phrase had its remarkable success in the world, powerful aesthetic interests were being satisfied by the conversion of a little-known poet into an English Laforgue; and the same interests demanded a catastrophic start to the modern world shortly after the death of Donne, and before *Paradise Lost*, that great dissociated poem which you must, said Mr. Eliot, read once for the meaning and once for the verse, and which is therefore of no use either to that illiterate audience he desiderates for his unified Symbolist poetry, or for the next best thing, a highly cultivated audience that also likes its art undissociated. The strangest irony in all this — and it is all I have to say about the second of these perverted poets — is that Milton, rather exceptionally, actually believed in and argued for the unity of the soul (a continuum of mind and sense), allowed his insistence on the inseparability of form and matter to lead him into heresy; and believed that poetry took precedence over other activities of the soul because it was simple (undissociated by intellect) sensuous and passionate. But this did not matter; there were overriding reasons why Milton had to be bent or broken. He was the main sufferer in the great experiment of projecting on to an historical scale a developed Romantic-Symbolist theory of the Image. And although, as Mr. Bateson has shown, Mr. Eliot borrowed the phrase 'dissociation of sensibility' from Gourmont's peculiar account of the processes of poetry in the mind of an individual (specifically Laforgue) and applied it to the history of a nation's poetry, it is obvious that behind the theory there is the whole pressure of the tradition I have been discussing. The historical effort of Symbolism has been to identify a period happily ignorant of the war between Image and discourse, an un-dissociated age. In the end, it is not of high importance that any age selected for this role is likely to be found wanting, except of course for the tendency to exclude particular poets and periods from the canon. Hulme could never have justified his selection; Pound was driven to Chinese, and a dubious theory of ideograms; Yeats believed his own theory only in a specially qualified way, admitting that its importance lay in the present and not in the past. This is true of Mr. Eliot also. The essays in which he proposed his theory represent a most fruitful and effective refinement of the Symbolist doctrine, yielding far more than Symons's, for instance, similar though they are in essentials. To attack his position has usually seemed to mean an assault on what most people are content to regard as the main tradition of modern verse.

One such attack, that of Mr. Yvor Winters, seems to me both extremely intelligent and extremely revealing; and it carries me on to the last phase of this essay, a cursory glance at the contemporary relation between Image and discourse. Mr. Winters looks for inconsistencies in Mr. Eliot's criticism, so that he can defend his own position, which is notoriously not a fashionable one. He insists that art is a statement of an understood experience, which it morally evaluates; and that poetry has, in consequence, the same *kind* of meaning as cruder statements of the same sort, so that one would expect it to be paraphrasable. This position is, of course, frankly opposed to a cherished Symbolist doctrine, and Mr. Winters is therefore very hostile to some of Eliot's opinions. For example, the famous sigh for an illiterate audience (analogous, by the way, to Yeats's desire for illiterate actors, and really a hopeless wish for an audience incapable of discourse and so cut off from intellection's universe of death) simply fans Winters' indignation, as does the cognate doctrine that meaning is only the burglar's bait for the housedog of intellect. So, when Eliot writes, in the beautiful essay on Dante, that "clear visual images are given much more intensity by having a meaning — we do not need to know what the meaning is, but in our awareness of the image we must be aware that the meaning is there too," and when Mr. Winters bullies him about this, we have a clear picture of the fundamental opposition between a Romantic-Symbolist criticism and a criticism conscientiously in reaction against it. Mr. Eliot says that a poem can be understood before its 'meaning' is taken, though the 'meaning' is not without importance. Winters replies: "If the meaning is important in the creation of the poem, at any rate, it is foolish to suppose that one can dispense with it in the reading of the poem or that the poet did not take his meaning seriously. Only the frailest barrier exists between the idea of this passage and Poe's theory that the poet should lay claim to a meaning when he is aware of none".

It is no use saying that Mr. Winters has simply misunderstood; he knows very well what Eliot means, as he shows when he traces Eliot's theory of necessary disorder in modern art to Romantic doctrines of organic form, and speaks of *The Waste Land* and *The Cantos* as belonging to the art of revery. He understands the roots of these poems, and even goes so far as to call Pound "a sensibility without a mind", which is, if nothing else, a very just punishment upon abusers of the word 'sensibility'. Mr. Winters, as we should expect, is eccentric in his choice of major modern poets, but he is nevertheless the only critic of any fame who can take for granted the history of the kind of poetry and criticism he is opposed to. In the essay on Eliot he bases a very important argument upon a revealing sentence which is hidden away in the introduction to the

Anabasis of St. Jean Perse: "There is a logic of the imagination as well as a logic of concepts". (We, I hope, understand what this means, and can see how sharply such a belief separates the modern from the 'Metaphysical' poet.) It is hard to resist Winters' argument that here "the word *logic* is used figuratively", that it indicates nothing but "qualitative progression", "graduated progression of feeling". Yet for all that the argument is false. It indicates no *progression* of any sort. Time and space are exorcised; the emblem of this 'logic' is the Dancer. This misunderstanding, slight as it seems, shows that the difference between these two critics is extremely wide. If you want to mean something, says Mr. Winters, you must mean it in the usual way; in other words, form is not significant. But to Mr. Eliot, and to many others, this is an admission that the speaker has no real notion at all of what art is. "People who do not appreciate poetry," says Mr. Eliot, "always find it difficult to distinguish between order and chaos in the arrangement of images." But Mr. Winters does appreciate poetry. The truth is that he is an anti-Symbolist critic, and this necessarily puts him in opposition to most of his contemporaries. For him, poetry is the impassioned expression on the countenance of *all* science and, as George Eliot called it, an aesthetic teacher. Since he does not believe that it deals in a different order of truth he has not the same difficulties about language, communication and paraphrase as the critics who oppose him.

I draw attention in this sketchy way to Mr. Winters, because he leads us to an understanding of what is one of the main issues of modern poetic. This is the unformulated quarrel between the orthodoxy of Symbolism and the surviving elements of an empirical-utilitarian tradition which, we are assured, is characteristically English. Yeats had a foot in both camps, the one stubbornly holding to the commonalty of the means of discourse and seeking to define those differences of degree which distinguish poetry, the other talking about images (sometimes indeed forgetting about words and their temporal behaviour altogether, or treating them as physical things like bits of string) and taking poetry to be a different kind of thing, a different mode of cognition, involving, at least as a working hypothesis, a different order of reality from any available to ordinary intellection. The difficulty of the first party is to find some way of talking about poetry and its propositions that does not disqualify it from the serious attention of *honnêtes gens*; for example, Richards's 'pseudo-statement' is asking for trouble, Wellek's theory of genre is too technical. On the other side, nobody can any longer (in the present state of semantics) be so offhand about the linguistic problems of the Image as the French Symbolists were. Indeed a good deal of the best modern criticism is interesting as evidence of the oscillations and tensions in the minds of critics between the claims of the Image and the claims of ordinary discourse.

These tensions are visible also in poetry, and it is possible that in the controlling of them the immediate future of our poetry lies, as well as our criticism and ways of looking at the past. At the moment, perhaps, the movement of the 'thirties away from aesthetic monism, the new insistence on the right to discourse, even to say such things as "We must love one another or die" (as Auden does in an exquisite poem) has ceased. There are good poets who cultivate a quasi-philosophical tone of meditation, but they are careful to have no design upon us, to place their meditation within the confines of reverie; there are others who prefer the ironies of stringently mechanical forms; but no Auden, nobody who wants, apparently, to go that way; and this is a pity. Recently Wallace Stevens has come to be more widely read in this country, and he is a poet who provides a unique, perhaps un-repeatable, solution to the image-and-discourse problem, by making the problem itself the subject of poems:

> Is the poem both peculiar and general?
> There's a meditation there, in which there seems
> To be an evasion, a thing not apprehended or
> Not apprehended well. Does the poet
> Evade us, as in a senseless element?
>
> Evade us, this hot, dependent orator,
> The spokesman at our bluntest barriers,
> Exponent by a form of speech, the speaker
>
> Of a speech only a little of the tongue?

One thing Stevens insists upon, and no poet is now likely to forget it: it is a lesson that Romantic aesthetic has taught once and for all. The poem is

Part of the *res* and not itself about it.
The poet speaks the poem as it is,
Not as it was.

Only by knowing this can the poet be "the necessary angel of the earth". The sentiment is Blake's, but it has become everybody's; yet Stevens's answer to the problem — it is the problem of dissociation — though very complete, and achieving in the late poem called 'The Rock' a most moving comprehensiveness, is not available to all poets, and they must seek their own.

Stevens's problems are the problems also of modern criticism (in its way and of necessity almost as obscure as the poetry). The unique power of the poet, however one describes it, is to make images or symbols, however one understands these, — as somehow visual, or, in the tradition of the new semantics, as the neologisms created by shifting contexts. How are these products related to discourse? Is there any way to talk of poetry without breaking up the monad and speaking of thought and image?

The one thing nearly everybody seems to be agreed upon is that the work of art has to be considered as a whole, and that considerations of 'thought' must be subordinated to a critical effort to see the whole as one image; the total work is not *about* anything / "a poem should not mean but *be*" — which is simply a vernacular way of saying what modern critics mean when they speak of it as 'autotelic' (they even speculate as to whether criticism is not also autotelic — the critic as artist once more). Put as simply as this, the position is not much changed since Mallarmé: "nul vestige d'une philosophie, l'éthique ou la métaphysique, ne transparaîtra; j'ajoute qu'il faut incluse et latente. . . le chant jaillit de source innée, antérieure à un concept". And many of the practical difficulties encountered by the holism of French Symbolism recur in modern critics. Take, for example, the problem which must sometimes arise, of what is the whole work of art. Is it the 'Voyage à Cythère' or is it the whole of *Les fleurs du Mal?* Is it 'They that have power to hurt' or the whole collection of Shakespeare's Sonnets? Professor Lehmann considers the first of these problems in his *Symbolist Aesthetic*, and seems to decide that the proper course is to take one poem at a time, since we know that

Les Fleurs du Mal is not "really a poem with a decisive organization overall" but "poems loosely strung on a string of predominating attitude". But how, it might be asked, can we be sure of this without trying the experiment of reading the whole book as a poem? Where do we get this important bit of information, which determines the whole question in advance? Certainly, on the purist view, from some illicit source — a knowledge of Baudelaire's intention. This may seem very extreme; but on the contrary it turns up with the regularity of an orthodoxy. We are told to read the whole of Shakespeare as one work. Mr. Wilson Knight reads all the Sonnets as one poem; he won his spurs by pioneering the Symbolist criticism of the plays, and is the most thoroughgoing of the holist Symbolist critics, unless we dare to say that Mr. Eliot, in his most famous essay, invites us to treat the whole of literature as one work.

There is a problem here, inherent in the Symbolist approach to poetry, which deserves more serious treatment than it gets, since it concerns the definition of what critics are talking about. In practice, of course, they cut the knot in silence, and assume the discontinuity of the poem they happen to be talking about, and even, for the purposes of exposition, talk about parts of poems as if they were wholes (just as they slyly paraphrase). Occasionally they even justify this practice. Mr. W. K. Wimsatt has several good things to say about the problem in his book *The Verbal Icon*, for instance this:

Extreme holism is obviously contrary to our experience of literature. (We do not wait until the end of the play or novel to know whether the first scene or chapter is brilliant or dull — no long work in fact would ever be witnessed or read if this were so.) A poem, said Coleridge, the father of holism in English criticism, is a composition which proposes "to itself such delight from the *whole*, as is compatible with a distinct gratification from each component part". The value of a whole poem, while undoubtedly reflecting something back to the parts, has to grow out of parts which are themselves valuable. *The Rape of the Lock* would not come off were not the couplets witty. We may add that good poems may have dull parts; bad poems, bright parts. How minutely this principle could be urged without arriving at a theory of Longinian "sudden flashes", of "cathartically charged images", of Arnoldian touchstones, of poetic diction, or of irrelevant local texture, I do not know. Nor what the minimal dimension of wit or local brilliance of structure may be; nor to what extent a loosely constructed whole may be redeemed by the energy of individual chapters or scenes. Yet the validity of partial value as a general principle in tension with holism seems obvious.

Something might be said against this defence of *littérature*, for the 'spatial' view of works of art, and it is worth considering that there are modern works (*Ulysses* is an obvious example) which are deliberately, and for long stretches, extremely tedious, and without any brilliance of local texture. Yet what Mr. Wimsatt says is satisfactory to common sense, and in fact modern holist criticism is closely related, so far as poetry is concerned, to that other Symbolist article which sets up the lyric poem as the norm, so that for the most part only short poems get the full treatment.

Even so, the question of how to treat partial aspects continues to rise and trouble practical critics, and occasionally provides new insights. Mr. Empson, for example, has developed a habit of referring regularly to the whole work in the discussions of its parts; Mr. Ransom has raised a whole theory upon the assertion that the value of 'texture' resides precisely in its irrelevance to the structural concern of the poem, and he is further heretical in allowing no poem to be without some embodied 'prose discourse', providing the logical relevance denied to the 'texture'. Mr. Winters is right, I think, when he calls this an embarrassing doctrine, holding that Ransom "does not know what to do with the rational content, how to account for it or evaluate it". (Mr. Winters of course does know this.) To put the matter so baldly is, of course, to do wrong to Mr. Ransom's intense though urbane efforts to solve an important problem; but my object here is merely to insist that the problem arises quite naturally out of the attempt (which must be made in any modern poetic) to find a place for discourse in a Symbolist poetry. Ransom accepts most of the Symbolist position, — he calls the poetry of the Image 'physical' and the poetry of discourse 'Platonic' — right down to the psychological theory of the artist as isolated or inhibited from action (the check on action he calls 'sensibility') and without a radical reorientation there is simply no room for discourse in the work of art so conceived. The problem comes up again in the associated criticism of Allen Tate. He also believes that art "has no useful relation to ordinary forms of action", and accepts a distinction similar to that of Ransom, finding the virtue of poetry in the *tension* between idea and image, or between abstraction and concretion, or between discourse and the symbol which can have no logical relation to it.

Such formulations, however fruitful they may be in the exegesis which stems from them (and it is arguable that they are not fruitful in this way at all) have the disadvantages, as well as the benefits, of their Romantic-Symbolist heritage. Mr. R. W. Stallman, in his useful account of these critics, asks us to distinguish between their "formalism" and "the aestheticism of the nineties"; but the differences are by no means as decisive as he suggests, and if one were able to construct a normal modern poetic it would be unlikely to contain much, apart from its semantic content, to surprise Arthur Symons. It is true that a new school of critics, the Chicago 'neo-Aristotelians', are directing us back to the *Poetics* and away from that preoccupation with metaphor (the rhetorical vehicle of the Image) which is an essential component of modern poetic, but one can truly say, without comment on the quality of this criticism, that, from the standpoint of modern orthodoxy, it is clearly tainted with heresy, the heresy of abstraction. What still prevails is the Symbolist conception of the work of art as aesthetic monad, as the product of a mode of cognition superior to, and different from, that of the sciences. Any alternative is likely to be treated as heretical — dubbed, for instance, 'ornamentalist', as degrading the status of the Image, and leading to another 'dissociation', another over-valuation of ideas in poetry similar to that effected by Hobbes. One result of this orthodoxy is that the practical business of criticism becomes enormously strenuous, despite the technical facilities provided by Richards and Empson; and that there is a good deal of what must be called cheating, for example in the matter of paraphrase. Good modern criticism is much more eclectic in method than most theoretical pronouncements suggest; it must not seem to believe in paraphrase (or, sometimes, in any form of historical approach to the work in question) yet these

157

and similar forbidden techniques are in fact frequently employed. It may be said that the strenuousness, as well as the obscurity, of such modern criticism, is a direct consequence of its Symbolist inheritance.

The effects of this inheritance may be traced also, so far as I know them, in the philosopher-aestheticians whom critics tend to take notice of (it would not be easy to say why they take notice of some and not of others). There are naturally many variations; but, to take two recent books, the 'concrete universal' as proposed by Mr. Wimsatt is the same thing as the Symbol of Mrs. Langer under a slightly different aspect. Mrs. Langer's is comfortably traditional in design, if not in execution. It starts from music, where the definition of symbol as "articulate but non-discursive form" does not raise the same problems of 'content' and 'ideas' as it does in literature; so far she shares the 'aestheticism' of the 'nineties'. (It is interesting, by the way, to find her quoting with approval a passage from Arthur Michel about the dance which would have pleased Mallarmé and Symons and Yeats — the dancer is conceived as oscillating "between two external poles of tension, thus transplanting the dancing body from the sensually existing atmosphere of materialism and real space into the symbolic supersphere of tension space"; and he speaks of "the dissolution of the dancer into swaying tension".) When she arrives at the problem of the discursive content of poems, Mrs Langer's answer is that "the poet uses discourse to create an illusion, a pure appearance, which is a non-discursive symbolic form". She distinguishes between this position and that of 'pure poetry' as formulated by Moore and Bremond, accurately calling the latter's a magical solution; it is magical in so far as it is Symbolist, and so, perhaps, in its different way, is hers. But hers is distinguished further by arduous and delightful discriminations. She gives modified approval to Mr. Pottle's view that "Poetry should be no purer than the purpose demands", but calls it a philosophical makeshift; exposes the mass of unphilosophical thinking that vitiates most attempts to distinguish between poetry and non-poetry; and argues that to maintain its interest in life poetry has to traffic with "serious thought". But "the framework of subject-matter" becomes part of the symbolic whole; something has to be *done* to it, it must, in the Croce-Collingwood sense, be 'expressed', and it will then be part of the work of art which is "a single indivisible symbol, although a highly articulated one".

Mrs. Langer has undoubtedly found a place for 'discourse' in het 'symbol' — so necessary, when the art is one which uses words — and the success of her books is probably an advance towards the dissociation of Romantic-Symbolist aesthetic from the anti-intellectualism with which it has been so persistently and inevitably associated from the beginning, and so potently since Rimbaud. An age of criticism, for so we tend to think of our epoch, is comforted by the assurance that reason can somehow get at poems, and that criticism itself should not be the autotelic act that Wilde as well as some later critics argued it must be (and as it indeed must, if art is the symbol by definition inexplicable). "The situation," says Mr. Wimsatt, "is something like this: In each poem there is something (an individual intuition — or a concept) which can never be expressed in other terms. It is like the square root of two or like pi, which cannot be expressed by rational numbers, but only as their *limit*. Criticism of poetry is like 1.414. . . or 3.1416. . ., not all it would be, yet all that can be had and very useful."

And this is all the critic can expect. He cannot give up the autonomy of the symbolic work of art, a concept of form which has been near the heart of criticism since Coleridge. And so he cannot expect ever to achieve finality in his own work; he is doomed to be limited, even if he remembers the symbolic origin of the discourse he is extracting for discussion. Not that a good critic would wish it otherwise; he is so accustomed to *defending* poetry on these very grounds, his way of thinking about poetry is, in fact, inclined to be defensive, and even when he is asserting poetry's unique powers there is likely to be a cautious anti-positivism in his tone. Reviewing Mr. Philip Wheelwright's recent book *The Burning Fountain*, Mr. M. H. Abrams points out that this excellent writer is "a prisoner of the theory he opposes" because he accepts the opposition between scientific and expressive language. And Mr. Abrams goes on to suggest, in a most sympathetic way, that we ought now to go over to the offensive. "An adequate theory of poetry must be constructed, not by a strategy of defense and limited counter-attack on grounds chosen by a different discipline, but by a positive strategy specifically adapted to disclose the special ends and structures and values, not only of poetry as such, but of the rich diversity of individual poems. What is needed is not merely a "metagrammar" and a "paralogic". What is needed, and what the present yeasty ferment in criticism may well portend, is simply, a poetic."

If such a poetic emerges it will still, of course, be Symbolist; but it will have a different place for discourse from any found for it during the nineteenth-century struggle with the positivists. It will owe much to modern semantics, but it will not call the discourse of poetry "pseudo-statement". Nor will its differences from scientific statement be reduced to differences of degree; it will not become statement transfigured by impassioned expression. The new poetic would be remote from the radicalism of Blake, have little to do with the forlorn hopes of Mallarmé, and less with the disastrous *derèglement* of Rimbaud. We have perhaps learnt to respect order, and felt on our bodies the effect of irrationalism, at any rate when the sphere of action is invaded by certain elements of the Romantic *rêve*. It will be a waking poetic, respecting order. "Shape' has no chance of interfering with 'form', to use Coleridge's distinction; but among good poets it never had. But 'reason' will return to poetics, and perhaps Mrs. Langer has shown how to find it a *modus vivendi* with the symbol. One notes also that Mr. Wimsatt, as his title suggests, is willing to allow both meanings of 'symbol' to the words of poetry, I mean those of the semasiologist and of the Romantic critic.

But in the end, of course, these matters are solved by poets and not by critics. That is why, I think, Yeats is so important in what I have been saying. He had a matured poet's concern for the relation of symbol to discourse. He understood that one pole of Symbolist theory is sacramentalism, whether Catholic or theurgic:

> Did God in portioning wine and bread
> Give man His thought, or his mere body?

and was willing to see in the discourse, whether of language or gesture, of the dedicated, symbolic values. He, as we have seen, most fully worked out the problems of the Image and of the nature of the poet's isolation; he understood the importance of magic to Symbolist aesthetic; and he also found his solution to that most urgent problem of discourse, assuming that such a statement as "The best lack all conviction", in contact with the vast image out of *Spiritus Mundi*, puts on the knowledge with the power of that image. So the slaves of time, the non-poets, will find a validity in his symbolic poems that is, for them, absent from the pure poetry of the dream. They share with the poet not only the Great Memory, but also the ordinary syntax of the daily life of action. Yeats's sun may be full of angels hymning Jehovah, but it is also a disc shaped somewhat like a guinea. This is not the dissociation of image that is complained of; it is an admission that art was always made *for* men who habitually move in space and time, whose language is propelled onward by verbs, who cannot always be asked to respect the new enclosure laws of poetry, or such forbidding notices as "No road through to action". Somehow, and probably soon, the age of dissociation — which is to say, the age that invented and developed the concept of dissociation — must end.

IX
CONCLUSION

I now see that the literary element in painting, the moral element in poetry, are the means whereby the two arts are accepted into the social order and become a part of life, and not things of the study and the exhibition.

YEATS

I have to admit that the last chapter gave no real notion of the variety and subtlety of modern criticism, nor of the impact upon it of precisely that interest the earlier Symbolists lacked, a systematic application to language-theory. The effect of this has certainly been to 'de-mythologise' Symbolism, to reconcile its Image with more empirical and utilitarian theories of language (as Richards's flux of interpenetrating elements is the language itself, rather than the intuitive order of Bergson and Hulme). The effort is to dispense with that supernaturalism that habitually, in one form or another, accompanies Symbolist theory — Boehme and the correspondences, magic and mediumship, the sacramentalism of some Roman Catholic aestheticians, like Mr. David Jones. It can now be admitted that words are not pictures, that words behave differently from things — although it might be argues that we now study the secret lives of words as if they were dreams, and restore to our theories of communication the essential Romantic magic, reducing our analogical universe to the language we speak. Nevertheless, the new attention to language has been anti-supernaturalist in effect. It has also

162

involved discriminations and definitions of the word 'symbol' itself which I have not gone into.

What remains clear, I hope, is that the twin concepts of the isolated artist and the supernatural Image to which he gains access, continue to be influential, and indeed stand behind these modern developments. I trust also that my focussing of the earlier part of the argument on Yeats has justified itself. He recommends himself for the part. His career continued, with no significant deviation, over the half century that separated the eighties from the outbreak of the last war; he spoke out; and he knew exactly the nature of his heritage. I think it would have been possible to put Mr. Eliot at the centre instead, and some points might have been more forcibly made by a discussion of the disposition of symbols in a work like *Ash Wednesday:* if the whole work is an image, how is it, to paraphrase Mrs. Langer, 'articulated'? But Eliot's relationship with discourse is less easy than that of Yeats. The problem is the same, and it is magnificently solved it is the problem of giving symbolic value to the 'sense', of identifying dancer and dance. But *Ash Wednesday* is, so to say, verbless, making no propositions and openly defying the intellect (though, not being illiterate, we all try to explicate what is by definition inexplicable). It is an arrangement of images, or an articulated image, requiring to be looked at 'spatially'. At the linguistic level Mr. Eliot has that precision of strange outline that all Symbolists require; nothing is more memorable in his verse than the immediate sense of exactness communicated, the impression of great resources of language delicately employed, and infinite flexibility of rhythm. And all this conveys the vitality of the Image, the movement in stillness and the life in death, without Yeats's concessions to the reader less privileged. Mallarmé would doubtless have been better pleased.

But Yeats is anxious that the poet should preserve his right to speak of his own part in the process of perception-creation, of the "private soul" which is "the sole source of pain"; and he is anxious that the reader should understand the relationship between the angels and the yellow disc. So, in 'Among Schoolchildren', he involves us in the children and their work, in the poet's self-deceptive pose, before he shows us how all this is related to the bronze and the marble, the dancer and the tree. Someone once said to me that another poet, Mr. Empson for instance, would have started this poem at the seventh stanza: "Both nuns and mothers worship images". The remnant would be an obscure but possible poem; but it would surely be a lesser one. The whole situation of the artist is relevant; the Image belongs to life in so far as the artist suffers for it. This suffering, as Mr. Eliot has said, is a private affair, and not in itself the reader's concern; as suffering, it ought not to be in the poetry (we remember the blank face and the drilled eyeball). But it can acquire a symbolic quality and be admitted; it is so in Wordsworth, it is so in Yeats; and, it must be confessed, in much of Eliot also. It is the additional explicitness, and the franker acknowledgment of ancestry in Yeats, that make him more helpful for my purposes.

It occurs to me that some readers might feel these purposes to be thwarted by the obsolescence of the idea of the difference of the artist, an idea which I confess to be essential to what I have been saying. If it were dead my remarks on the place of the Image in our own time would of course have to be qualified. It is probably true that the number of poets who can work only by artificial light with a gun on the desk, or when drunk, or with much recourse to rash encounters under the iron lilies of the Strand, is now rather small, and it is a common complaint that poets look like bank-clerks. But all this has nothing to do with the truth that poets continue to conceive of themselves as different, isolated, as a necessary preliminary to the achievement of a truth which, though it must use the dialect of the tribe, yet fanatically purifies it. Art for art's sake is a derisory sentiment, yet questions of the morality of the work will usually be answered in terms of its perfection, not of its 'message'. The immorality of art is the kind of corruption (a highly special concept) that Collingwood speaks of, not the sort detected and prosecuted by the police. The utter failure of the propaganda poetry of the thirties to survive (look, for example, at Auden's *Spain*, a poem once greatly admired and now embarrassing) is proof that we still cannot bear poetry that has a design upon us. Its design must still be upon a truth which is not relative or customary, but finite and knowable in terms of the Image. For the same reason we continue to revere metaphor, though we all know how incurably metaphoric is our whole system of communication. We continue also to revere the maker of metaphor for his special *acutezza*, which enables him to pierce the veil; and to allow that this power must, in terms of life, be an expensive one.

No criticism of this kind ever changed so much as a poem, though it sometimes appears to do so by the accident of getting written by poets who are doing something new; so it would be more presumptuous than profitable for me to attempt positive recommendations. My main business has been what, in discussing Hulme, I called the commendable one of revising historical categories. But as no historian, however tentative, can be denied his *utinam*, however useless, I will risk a final word on what I should like to see happening.

Symbolist criticism has always acknowledged — and without such an acknowledgment it is impossible to conceive of the success of a literary movement — the importance of the poetry of the past to the new poetry. The further admission, discussed in the previous chapter, that discourse may be domesticated in the articulated symbolism of the work of art, automatically overthrows the doctrine of the supremacy of the short poem, and the modern novel further demonstrates the possibilities of complex symbolic relations in long works. The next step, perhaps, is to make available some of the poetry of the past which has been excluded by earlier Symbolist assumptions, and above all, to restore the long poem to the centre of activity. For the English this means Milton; and this fact alone justifies any attempt to kill the Symbolist historical doctrine of dissociation of sensibility as publicly as possible. The liberation of Milton — it has begun, but has not got far enough as yet — from that ban under which he has remained, at any rate in the eyes of many young poets, throughout the present century, is of extreme importance to the future. Spenser needs liberating, too; but Milton is more important. There are fewer flats among the elevations, far less 'binding-matter' in *Paradise Lost*, than is habitually assumed, even by people who read Milton. The time cannot be far off when it will be read once more as the most perfect achievement of English poetry, perhaps the richest and most intricately beautiful poem in the world. When it does, poets will marvel that it could have been done without so long; as easy, they will say, to imagine a Greek literature which abjured Homer.

There seems no good reason why this development should necessitate the end of the vogue for Donne and the Metaphysicals; yet there are signs already that it is ending, like the older taste for Jacobean drama. For this we must thank the Symbolist device of placing Donne and Milton on an historical seesaw. It is a great pity because at this moment it is possible — so fully has Grierson's work been supplemented — to read Donne more accurately than ever before; and because the chance of a significant revaluation of a great neglected poet like Jonson, and a fine neglected dramatist like Middleton, must go too. But these losses we will sustain more cheerfully if they are merely the price of Milton's restoration, if we can see him again as not an obstruction but a model. It may seem that I am calling up a ghastly rhetoric from the grave; but we are apt to be misled by Verlaine's remark. He too has his rhetoric, and as long as there is verbal communication there will be rhetorics; they are the means to order, and without that no lamp burns in the tower, no dancer spins. If poets turn back to Milton they will forget the old hatred of his rhetoric or his theology or (easiest, surely, of all) his life, and discover, if I may use the lines eulogistically, 'mere' now meaning 'pure', that

> He has found, after the manner of his kind,
> Mere images.

And by the time they have done that, the dissociation of sensibility, the great and in some ways noxious historical myth of Symbolism (though the attempt to see history in terms of the Image was noble) will be forgotten, except by historians crying their new categories and still unheard persuasions.

INDEX

Abrams, M. H., *The Mirror and the Lamp* vii, 93, 95; 159.
Adams, Henry, 59, 143.
Agrippa, Cornelius, 109.
Alison, Archibald, 93.
Aristotle, *Poetics* 157.
Arnold, Matthew, 6, 11, 12ff., 24, 66, 96, 110, 156; *Empedocles on Etna* 12ff; 'The Strayed Reveller' 14; 'Obermann', 'Obermann once more' 14; *Preface* of 1853 12.
Auden, W. H., 153; *Spain* 164.
Augustine, St., 126.
Averroes, 142.

Bacon, Francis, 92, 142.
Balzac, Honoré de, 117-8; *Le Chef d'oeuvre inconnu* 63, 117f.; *Séraphitâ* 112.
Bateson, F. W., 147, 150.
Baudelaire, Charles, 5, 63, 111, 112, 120, 131; 'Voyage à Cythère' 154-5.
Beardsley, Aubrey, 74.
Beerbohm, Max, 65.
Beethoven, 6.
Béguin, A., *L'Ame romantique et le rêve* vii, 4, 14, 116.
Bergson, Henri, 47, 121ff., 126, 128, 129, 130, 131, 133, 134, 135, 136, 144, 162; *Introduction to Metaphysics* 121.
Bion, 36.
Blackmur, R. P., *Language as Gesture* 22.
Blake, William, 5, 12, 14, 26, 33, 34, 41f., 44, 45, 47, 51, 56, 57, 58, 59, 60, 66, 82, 89, 92, 93, 94, 100ff., 107, 108, 109, 110, 111, 112, 113, 130, 148, 154, 160; *Poetical Sketches* 96; 'Love and Harmony combine' 96-7; *The Laocoon Group* 97; *Vision of the Last Judgment* 113; Yeats's edition of 49.
Blin, G., on Baudelaire, 111.
Boehme, J., 5, 109, 111.
Bremond, Henri, 158.
Bridges, Robert, 149; 'Eros' 58.
Brooke, Rupert, 149.
Brooke, Stopford, 148.
Brooks, Cleanth, 116.
Browning, R., 139.
Buffet, Bernard, 3f.
Burke, Edmund, 96.
Burns, Robert, 10.
Burton, Robert, 8.

Calvert, Edward, 33, 34, 35, 41, 42, 45, 102.
Campbell, J., 'The Dancer' 58.
Capellanus, Andreas, 142.
Carlyle, Thomas, 'Hero as Poet' 95; *Sartor Resartus* 109.
Catullus, 63, 146.
Cavalcanti, Guido, 136, 140, 144, 146.
Chapman, George, 139.
Cino da Pistoia, 140, 144.
Coleridge, S. T., 8, 11, 14, 15, 21, 26, 44, 45, 46, 47, 59, 66, 72, 93, 95, 96, 100, 110, 113, 125, 126, 127, 148, 155, 159, 160; 'Ode: Dejection' 6, 10, 89ff; 'Ancient Mariner' 9; *Biographia Literaria* 9, 72, 93; *Statesman's Manual*, 94.

Collingwood, W. G., *Principles of Art* 12, 49, 101, 158, 164.

Crashaw, Richard, 149.

Cremonini, Cesare, 142.

Croce, G., 158.

Courthope, W. J., *History of English Poetry* 148.

Cowley, Abraham, 149; 'On the Death of Mr. William Hervey' 38ff.

Dante, 33, 53, 64, 140, 144.

Darwin, Charles, 92.

Descartes, 48, 125, 142.

Dryden, John, 140.

Dickens, C., *Little Dorrit* 5.

Donne, John, 27, 49, 53, 54, 59, 107, 114, 131, 139, 146ff., 165f.

Dowson, Ernest, 22, 24.

Duncan, J. E., 148.

Dürer, 8, 57.

Eliot, George, 11, 66, 148, 152.

Eliot, T. S., 44, 48, 119, 120, 138ff, 147, 148, 149, 150, 151, 155, 163, 164; 'Mr. Prufrock' 56; 'The Metaphysical Poets' 139f.; 'Milton' 139f.; *Dante* 151; *Anabasis of St.-J. Perse* 152; *Ash Wednesday* 163.

Empson, W., 156, 157, 163-4.

Fairlie, Barker, *Heine* 67.

Fenellosa, Ernest, 78, 136.

Ficino, Marsilio, 8.

Flaubert, G., 68, 74.

Flecker, J. E., 'A Queen's Song' 87f.

Ford, Ford Madox, 121, 135.

Fuller, Loïe 71.

Gautier, Théophile de; 120; *Mlle. de Maupin* 61.

Gilson, Etienne, *History of Christian Philosophy in the Middle Ages* 142.

Godwin, William, *St. Leon* 7.

Goethe, *Wilhelm Meister* 94.

Gosse, Edmund, 149.

Gourmont, Rémy de, 100, 120, 130, 150.

Gregory, Lady, 30ff, 35; *Kinkora* 33; *Image* 33.

Gregory, Robert, 26, 30ff.

Grierson, H. J. C., ed. of Donne 147, 148, 166.

Grosart, A. 149; ed. of Donne 148.

Guérin, Maurice de, 14, 41.

Guinicelli, 140.

Hallam, A., 96.

Hartley, David, 93, 125.

Hazlitt, 7, 93.

Heine, H., 67f., 71; *Die Bäder von Lucca* 67f.; *Florentinische Nächte* 67f., 'Atta Troll' 75.

Henley, W. E., 22.

Herbert of Cherbury, Lord, 139, 142.

Herder, J. G., 95, 96; *On the knowledge and feeling of the human soul* 95.

'Hermes Trismegistus', 109.

Hobbes, Thomas, 157.

Homer, 33, 96.

Hone, J., *W. B. Yeats* 31, 81.

Hough, Graham, *The Last Romantics* 21.

Hugo, Victor, 5, 49.

Hulme, T. E., 28, 55, 92, 93, 119-137, 143, 144, 145, 150, 162, 165; *Speculations* 119ff; translation of Bergson's *Introduction to Metaphysics* 121, 'Cinders' 130; 'Notes on Language and Style' 131.

Husserl, E., 122.

Huxley, T. H., 92.

Huysmans, J. K., 3, 41, 73, 109, 116; *A Rebours* 68.

Ibsen, 46.

Innes, J. D., 32, 33.

James, H., 2, 22-3; *The Lesson of the Master* 22; 'The Art of Fiction' 12.

Jeffares, N., 88.

John, Augustus, 57.

'John, Evan', 'Herodiade' 74.

Johnson, Lionel, 22, 23f., 38, 41, 42; 'Mystic and Cavalier' 24.

Jones, David, 162.
Jonson, Ben, 166.
Joyce, James, *Portrait of the Artist as a Young Man* 1, 2, 45, 53, 102; *Ulysses* 156.

Keats, J., 7, 12, 21, 67; 'Ode to Melancholy' 8; *Hyperion* 8ff; *Lamia* 8.
Kenner, H., *The Poetry of Ezra Pound* 135.
Kierkegaard, S., 6, 14, 66.
Knight, G. Wilson, 155.

Laforgue, J., 114, 119, 149, 150.
Langer, Susanne, *Feeling and Form* 158-9, 160, 163.
Lawrence, D. H., 6.
Lehmann, A. G., *The Symbolist Aesthetic in France* vii, 119, 132, 154.
Leonardo da Vinci, 47.
Lewis, C. Day, 138.
Lewis, Wyndham, vii, 60, 133ff, 138; BLAST 134-5.
Lichtenberg, G. C., 4.
Lipps, Theodor, 122.
Locke, J., 92, 93.
'Longinus', 155, 156.

Maeterlinck, M., 74, 109, 115.
Maistre, J. de, 112.
Mallarmé, S., 70, 79, 85-6, 109-110, 114ff, 117, 120, 130-1, 136, 154, 158, 160, 163; *Hérodiade* 68f.; *L'Après-midi d'un Faune* 114; *Un Coup de Dès* 115; *Divagations* 71, 117.
Mann, Thomas, 12, 64; *Death in Venice* 2; *Tonio Kröger* 2.
Marino, G. B., 62.
Martial, 40.
Mencken, H. L., 6.
Meynell, Mrs., 149.
Michel, André, 158.
Michelangelo, 25, 53, 54, 124.
Middleton, T., 166.
Mill, J. S., 21-2.
Milton, 36, 139, 140, 146ff., 149, 150, 165-6; *Paradise Lost* 166.

Montaigne, 20, 125.
Moore, George, 43, 158.
Moore, G. E., 122.
Moreau, G., 68, 73, 74, 75; 'Salomé dansant devant Hérode' 68f.
Moritz, K. P., 29.
Murger, H., 3.

Nerval, G. de, 109, 111, 116; *Le Rêve et la Vie* 111.
Newton, Isaac, 92.
Nō drama, 77ff.
Novalis, F. von H., 112.

O'Shaughnessy, A., 66; 'The Daughter of Herodias' 74.

Palmer, Samuel, 26, 33, 34, 41, 45, 102.
Pascal, 20, 121, 122, 123, 125, 126.
Pater, Walter, 2, 3, 5, 12, 15, 17, 19ff., 29, 58, 62, 63, 66, 67, 100, 107, 126, 131, 134, 137, 148; *Marius the Epicurean* 11f., 20f., 24; *The Renaissance* 11f., 114; 'The Child in the House' 63; 'Emerald Uthwart' 64, 65, 134.
Petrarch, 136, 144, 146.
Plato, 93.
Plomer, William, 'A Levantine' 58.
Poe, E. A., 117, 151.
Poizat, A., *Le Symbolisme de Baudelaire à Claudel* 117.
Pomponazzi, 142.
Pope A., 19; *Essay on Man* 125; *The Rape of the Lock* 155.
Pottle, F. A., *The Idiom of Poetry* 158.
Pound, Ezra, 44, 48, 55, 78, 85, 100, 119ff., 133ff., 143ff., 148, 150; *Cantos* 63, 118, 136, 137; *Make It New* 143f.
Praz, M., *The Romantic Agony* vii, 60f., 68, 74.

Quinn, J., 32.

Ransom, John Crowe, 156f.
Read, Sir H., 132; editor of Hulme's *Speculations* 121.

Richards, I. A., 3, 132f., 153, 157, 162; *Principles of Literary Criticism* 67; *Philosophy of Rhetoric* 132.

Ricketts, C., 33, 74.

Rimbaud, 114, 120, 159, 160.

Roberts, Michael, *T. E. Hulme* 121, 125.

Rodenbach, G., 71.

Rossetti, D. G., 15, 61, 64, 65, 67, 131, 135; 'Lilith' 61f.

Rousseau, 125.

Sainte-Beuve, 19.

Schelling, 149.

Schlegel, 46, 47.

Schopenhauer, 125, 130, 136.

Sēami, *Kwadensho* 78.

Sénancour, 14, 19; *Obermann* 13.

Shakespeare, *Sonnets* 154.

Shaw, G. B., *Candida* 23, 33.

Shelley, 8, 22, 33, 36.

Sidney, Sir P., 37.

Sorel, 144.

Spenser, 35, 36, 131, 165.

Spinoza, 139.

Stallman, R. W., *Critiques and Essays in Criticism, 1920-1948* 157.

Stevens, Wallace, 153f.; 'Anecdote of a Jar' 47f.; 'The Rock' 154.

Strauss, Richard, 73.

Sturge Moore, 56, 58, 87, 88.

Swedenborg, 5, 109, 111.

Swinburne, 61.

Symons, Arthur, 6, 65, 66, 68, 70, 100, 107-118, 119, 148, 149, 150, 158; 'To a Dancer' 70; 'Javanese Dancers' 70; 'La Mélinite: Moulin Rouge' 70; *Spiritual Adventures* 72f.; 'The World as Ballet' 72f; *William Blake* 107, 110; *The Symbolist Movement in Literature* 107ff.

Synge, J. M., *Deirdre of the Sorrows* 33, 38.

Taine, 109.

Tasso, 62.

Tate, Allen, 157.

Taupin, René, 120.

Tennyson, 139; *In Memoriam* 62.

Theocritus, 36.

Thompson, Francis, 149.

Thornton, R. J., translation of Virgil, 33.

Titian, 7, 27, 54, 59.

Toulouse-Lautrec, 71.

Tucker, Abraham, 93.

Turnell, Martin, *Baudelaire* 5.

Turner, W. J., 'The Dancer' 58.

Tuve, Rosemond, *Elizabethan and Metaphysical Imagery* 147.

Tynan, Kathleen, 51.

Ure, Peter, *Towards a Mythology* 37.

Verlaine, 33, 35, 50, 51, 62, 63, 65, 97, 108, 114, 120, 137, 166.

Villiers de l'Isle Adam, 7, 114.

Virgil, 33, 35, 36, 146.

Wagner, Geoffrey, 134.

Wagner, Richard, 42, 77.

Warren, A. H., *English Poetic Theory 1825-65* 95-6.

Webster, John, 114.

Wellek, R., *Theory of Literature* 153.

Wheelwright P., *The Burning Fountain* 159.

Wilde, Oscar, 6, 12, 15, 22, 27, 46, 66, 68, 75, 133, 159; 'The Critic as Artist' 44f.; *Salome* 73, 74; 'Helen' 74; 'The Sphinx' 74.

Wimsatt, W. K., *The Verbal Icon* 155-6, 158, 159, 160.

Witt, Marion, 34, 37, 40, 42.

Winters, Yvor, 150ff, 156-7.

Wordsworth, 10, 12, 15, 21, 45, 92, 93, 101, 127, 164; *Preface to Lyrical Ballads* 10; 'The Ruined Cottage' 11; *The Prelude* 11; 'Resolution and Independance' 11, 33, 34, 41, 48, 101; *Guilt and Sorrow* 93; *Preface* of 1815, 127.

Worringer, Wilhelm, *Abstraktion und Einfühlung* 122ff., 126, 134.

Yeats, J. B., 25, 30, 61.

Yeats, W. B., 2, 6, 7, 11, 12, 15, 18, 19, 22, 23, 24, 27, 31, 32-4, 36, 43, 44, 45, 46, 48, 49, 56, 58, 68,

73, 74, 75ff., 82, 86ff., 96, 100, 101, 107, 108, 112, 120, 131, 133, 134, 143, 145, 148, 150, 151, 158, 160f., 162, 163, 164; *Autobiographies passim; A Vision* 24, 26, 27, 55, 59, 75, 76, 81; edition of Blake 100, 111; *The Celtic Twilight* 27; *Per Amica Silentia Lunae* 28; *Ideas of Good and Evil* 51, 97, 110; 'Red Hanrahan' 27; 'Poetry and the Tradition' 27; 'Symbolism in Painting' 34, 101-2; 'Symbolism in Poetry' 102; *Observer* obituary of Robert Gregory 32-4; *Discoveries* 49; 'The Guitar Player' 49ff, 97; 'The Looking Glass' 49ff.; 'The Tree of Life' 97; 'The Tragic Theatre' 77; 'Certain Noble Plays of Japan' 79; 'The Second Coming' 17; 'In Memory of Major Robert Gregory' 30-42; 'Shepherd and Goatherd' 35, 36; 'An Irish Airman foresees his death' 37; 'The Tower' 38; 'A Prayer for my Daughter' 38, 58, 99; 'The Statues' 59, 135; 'Super-

natural Songs' 59, 81; 'The Double Vision of Michael Robartes' 59, 60; 'Michael Robartes and the Dancer' 52, 160; 'Adam's Curse' 55; 'A Crazed Girl' 58f.; 'Wisdom' 64; 'The Hosting of the Sidhe' 74; *The Wind Among the Reeds* 74; 'Nineteen Hundred and Nineteen' 76; 'Among Schoolchildren' 83ff., 91, 163; 'The Living Beauty' 84; 'Vacillation' 86; 'A Dialogue of Self and Soul' 86; 'The Choice' 86; 'Sailing to Byzantium' 87ff.; 'Byzantium' 87ff.; *The Winding Stair* 87; 'The Circus Animal's Desertion' 89f.; *The Wanderings of Oisin* 89; *The Rose* 96; 'The Two Trees' 96; *Resurrection* 24; *The Shadowy Waters* 33; *At The Hawk's Well* 80, 83; *The Only Jealousy of Emer* 80; *A Full Moon in March* 80f.; *The King of the Great Clock Tower* 81; *The Herne's Egg* 82; *Purgatory* 82; *The Death of Cuchulain* 82; *The Countess Cathleen* 89.

ARK PAPERBACKS

CLAUDE LÉVI-STRAUSS
THE BEARER OF ASHES

Claude Lévi-Strauss is one of the intellectual giants of the twentieth century, a leading exponent of structuralism and a great social anthropologist. Yet he is a very private and isolated figure who has been reticent about himself, and this revealing book provides a fascinating insight into Lévi-Strauss's character through a careful reading of the more speculative passages of his books and interviews. It is a very readable introduction to Lévi-Strauss and his work, which places the world-view of this great French writer in the context of twentieth-century intellectuals' struggles to come to grips with cultural relativism and the problem of the primitive.

Claude Lévi-Strauss is Professor of Social Anthropology at the Collège de France. His publications include *The Elementary Structures of Kinship* (1949), *Tristes Tropiques* (1955), *The Savage Mind* (1962) and *Introduction to a Science of Mythology* (1969–79; 4 volumes).

DAVID PACE

David Pace is Associate Professor in the Department of History and Western European Studies, Indiana University.

United Kingdom £3.95 net

ARK PAPERBACKS

ONE-DIMENSIONAL MAN

Marcuse argues that modern society - but mainly those societies recognized as most liberal - is intolerably repressive. He believes that the one small hope of improvement lies in some revolutionary elite which may force the 'unenlightened' to be free.

'Professor Marcuse is out not only to interpret the world but also to change it. He brings to the task an equipment rarely found among professional philosophers and an idiom – Hegelian, Marxist and Freudian – that is altogether his own. In the tradition of Karl Mannheim he attempts a diagnosis of our times – something which social scientists and philosophers today abjure. It is also a polemic *with* our times, a steady often repetitive condemnation.' – *Encounter*

HERBERT MARCUSE

Herbert Marcuse (1898–1979) was born and educated in Berlin. In 1934 he left Nazi Germany, and took refuge in the USA, where he taught at Columbia University. He then held appointments at Harvard, Brandeis and at the University of California at San Diego, becoming known in the 1960s as the official ideologue of 'campus revolutions' in the USA and in Europe. His books include *Reason and Revolution* (1941), *Eros and Civilization* (1955), *Soviet Marxism* (1958) and *One-Dimensional Man* (1964), his most popular and most influential work.

United Kingdom £3.95 net
ISBN 0-7448-0040-4

ARK PAPERBACKS

PSYCHOLOGICAL REFLECTIONS

Carl Gustav Jung was one of the great thinkers of our time. In the course of his long medical practice he reflected deeply on human nature and human problems, and his prolific writings bear witness to his extraordinary wisdom and insight. This anthology of his writings is the perfect introduction to Jung's works, for the general reader as well as for the student of analytical psychology. It contains nearly thirteen hundred quotations from over one hundred works, arranged under four main headings:

The Nature and Activity of the Psyche
Man in His Relation to Others
The World of Values
On Ultimate Things.

C. G. JUNG

C. G. Jung (1875-1961), the Swiss psychiatrist and founder of Analytical Psychology, was an original thinker who made an immense contribution to the understanding of the human mind. In his early years he was a lecturer in psychiatry at the University of Zürich, and collaborated with Sigmund Freud. He gave up teaching to devote himself to his private practice in psychiatry and to research. He travelled widely and was a prolific author, often writing on subjects other than analytical psychology, such as mythology, alchemy, flying saucers and the problem of time. Jung was also responsible for defining such influential and widely-used terms as the Collective Unconscious, Extraversion/Introversion and Archetypes.

United Kingdom £3.95 net

ARK PAPERBACKS

WORKING WITH STRUCTURALISM

'This is a sane, highly intelligent, lucidly written book, and one which everyone concerned with literature must read at least once.' – Christopher Stace, *Daily Telegraph*

David Lodge is actively involved in university teaching, academic criticism, literary journalism and novel writing; this book reflects his concern to preserve the connection and continuity between these different discourses.

His discussion ranges from Thomas Hardy to Tom Wolfe and from the poetics of fiction to the poetry of Psychobabble. His work applies directly to structuralist methods of analysis, and the book as a whole aims to demonstrate the possibility of working with structuralism in the sense of working alongside it, recognizing its existence as a fact of intellectual life without being totally dominated by it.

DAVID LODGE

David Lodge is Professor of Modern English Literature at the University of Birmingham. He is also a novelist, and his books include *Changing Places* (1975), *How Far Can You Go?* (1980) and *Small World* (1984). His numerous critical publications include *Language of Fiction* (1966) and *Novelist at the Crossroads* (1971).

ISBN 0-7448-0043-9

United Kindom £3.95 net